T0003034

# THIS
# BOOK
## WILL
## (HELP)
# COOL
### THE
# CLIMATE

Visit us on the Web! rhcbooks.com

Educators and librarians, for a variety of teaching tools, visit us at RHTeachersLibrarians.com

Library of Congress Cataloging-in-Publication Data is available upon request.
ISBN 978-0-593-30870-7 (hardcover) | ISBN 978-0-593-30871-4 (lib. bdg.) |
ISBN 978-0-593-30872-1 (ebook)

Printed in Canada
10 9 8 7 6 5 4 3 2 1
First American Edition

# THIS BOOK WILL (HELP) COOL THE CLIMATE

## 50 WAYS TO CUT POLLUTION AND PROTECT OUR PLANET!

### ISABEL THOMAS
### ILLUSTRATED BY ALEX PATERSON

RANDOM HOUSE 🏠 NEW YORK

# CONTENTS

1. **KNOW** your **PLANET** .............. 10

2. **KNOW** your **ENEMY** ............. 15

3. **DENY** the **DENIERS** ............. 19

4. **EAT** your **NEIGHBORS** ............. 22

5. **TURN GARBAGE** into **GROCERIES** ............. 25

6. **TINKER TRAINING** ............. 27

7. **START** an **ECO-LIBRARY** ......... 32

8. **REWILD** your **BACKYARD** ...... 36

9. **BE MORE GRETA** ............. 40

10. **STAY OUT** of **HOT WATER** ...... 44

11. **SAY NAY** TO THE **SPRAY** . . . . . . . . . 49

12. **TAKE** A **STAYCATION** . . . . . . . 52

13. **MEASURE** YOUR **FEET** . . . . . . . . 55

14. **DON'T FEED** YOUR **TRASH CAN** . . . 59

15. **PROCRASTINATE** FOR
THE **PLANET** . . . . . . . . . . . . . . . . . . 62

16. **GROW** A **FREE TREE!** . . . . . . . . . 65

17. **STOP** **RECYCLING** . . . . . . . . . . . 68

18. **BEAT** THE **JARGON** . . . . . . . . . . . 71

19. **MAKE** YOUR **CLOTHES**
**IMMORTAL** . . . . . . . . . . . . . . . . . . 76

20. **UPDATE** YOUR **PLATE** . . . . . . . . . 80

21. **TAKE IT** from a **T. REX** . . . . . . . . . . . . . 86

22. **PEE** on the **COMPOST PILE!** . . . 89

23. **UNPLUG** for the **PLANET** . . . . . . . 92

24. **BREAK** the **FASHION RULES** . . . . 95

25. **ASSIGN** your **SCHOOL**
    **SOME HOMEWORK** . . . . . . . . . . . . . 99

26. **DON X-RAY SPECS** . . . . . . . . . . 104

27. **ASK AWKWARD QUESTIONS** . . . 108

28. **ACT LIKE IT'S** an
    **EMERGENCY** . . . . . . . . . . . . . . . 112

29. **DON'T GET TOO DRAINED** . . . . . 115

30. **INVITE** an **EXPERT** . . . . . . . . . . . 119

31. **AVOID FOUR WHEELS** . . . . . . . . . 122

32. **CAST** YOUR **VOTE** . . . . . . . . . . . . . . 125

33. **LIVE S-L-O-W-L-Y** . . . . . . . . . . . . . . 129

34. **SUSS OUT** THE
**SCIENCE SUPERPOWERS** . . . . . . 132

35. **GIVE SIGHTS, SOUNDS, AND
SENSATIONS . . . NOT STUFF!** . . . 135

36. **OPEN** A **MUSEUM** . . . . . . . . . . . 138

37. **CLEAR** OUT THE **CLUTTER** . . . . . . . 141

38. **HACK** YOUR **HOME** . . . . . . . . . . . . 144

39. **PARK** AND **STRIDE** . . . . . . . . . . . 148

40. **TACKLE CARBON
PAWPRINTS** . . . . . . . . . . . . . . . . 152

41. **BE ANNOYING** . . . . . . . . . . . . . . . 155

42. **LETTERS** for **CHANGE** . . . . . . . . . 157

43. **FILL** your **HOME**
    with **SNAKES** . . . . . . . . . . . . . . . 161

44. **MARCH** for the **CLIMATE** . . . . . . 165

45. **SWAP** your **STUFF** . . . . . . . . . . . 169

46. **LEAD** by **EXAMPLE** . . . . . . . . . 172

47. **HUNT** for your **HERO** . . . . . . . . 174

48. **DON'T TRY** to be **PERFECT** . . . . 178

49. **SHARE** a **STORY** . . . . . . . . . . . 180

50. **GREEN, SLEEP, REPEAT** . . . . . . 184

**INDEX** . . . . . . . . . . . . . . . 188

# QUICK GUIDE TO THE

# PLANET-O-METER

## SAVES:

**WILDLIFE**

**PAPER/WOOD**

**ELECTRICITY**

**WASTE**

**RAIN FOREST**

**POLLUTION**

**FOSSIL FUEL**

**WATER**

**FOOD**

**IMPACT:**    **COST:**    **DIFFICULTY:**

# KNOW YOUR PLANET

Knowledge is your number one weapon in the fight against climate change. Let's start by finding out what's so special about Earth's climate.

**PLANET-O-METER**

If you could choose to live **ANYWHERE** in our solar system, you'd probably still pick Earth. While parts of our planet can get as toasty as 136.4° Fahrenheit (F) or as ch-ch-chilly as −126.4°F, the average surface temperature is a comfortable 59°F. Compare this to Mars, with an average temperature of −81.4°F, and it's easy to see why we stay put!

Earth's temperature is just right for living things, and not only because of our prime position in the solar system. After all, Earth and the moon are roughly the same distance from the sun, and yet from day to night the moon's surface temperature swings between −279.4°F and 260.6°F. The secret to Earth's success is our atmosphere—the thin layer of air around the planet. This atmosphere is a mixture of various gases:

NITROGEN

OXYGEN

ARGON

WATER VAPOR

CARBON DIOXIDE

NEON

HELIUM

METHANE

KRYPTON

HYDROGEN

NITROUS OXIDE

XENON

OZONE

Some of these gases—especially water vapor, carbon dioxide, methane, and nitrous oxide—are known as greenhouse gases, because they trap some of the sun's energy as heat. Step inside a greenhouse and you'll notice a **BIG** temperature difference between the air inside and outside. The glass walls and roof of a greenhouse are good at letting sunlight in, which warms up everything inside. But the glass is bad at letting this heat out again. The air inside the greenhouse becomes so warm that it creates a different climate—one where all sorts of plants thrive. Greenhouse gases work in a similar way on a much bigger scale, keeping the whole planet warmer than it would otherwise be.

The natural greenhouse effect is a good thing. It stops the energy that reaches Earth from escaping back into space (like it does on the moon), making life on Earth possible. Without the greenhouse gases in our atmosphere, the average temperature on Earth would be around −0.4° to −9.4°F!

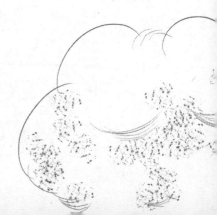

But a few decades ago, scientists noticed something worrying. The greenhouse effect is increasing, trapping more of the sun's energy than normal. Around the world, each of the last three decades has been warmer than **ANY** other decade in the past 170 years. In the United States, for example, the average January temperature from 1991 to 2020 was 32.35°F, compared to an average of 30.13°F for the 20th century. A similar average rise has been measured around the world. These aren't just the findings of one or two scientists, but **THOUSANDS** of studies.

Earth's average surface temperature
has risen by almost 2°F since 1800,
when recordkeeping began.

A 2°F temperature rise doesn't **SOUND** too bad, but it's not just Earth's average temperature that's changing. Earth's water and weather cycles are driven by the sun's energy. Global warming has already changed patterns of local weather conditions. Northern Europe and parts of Asia and North America have become wetter since 1900, with less snow and heavier rainstorms. At the same time, parts of Africa, the Mediterranean, and Asia have become drier. In the Arctic (where temperatures are rising faster than everywhere else), less sea ice has formed every winter since 1979. Glaciers around the world are shrinking as their ice melts more quickly than normal. The same is happening to the huge ice sheets that cover Greenland and Antarctica. All this melted ice has to go somewhere, and between 1901 and 2010, the average global sea level rose by 7.5 inches.

Armed with these facts, you'll be able to explain to anyone that there's no doubt that global warming and climate change have already happened. But will the temperature and the sea level keep rising? To answer that, you need to know what turbocharged the greenhouse effect in the first place.

# KNOW YOUR ENEMY

When scientists notice something as weird and as worrying as global warming, they work as detectives to find out what's going on.

**PLANET-O-METER**

If we think about global warming as a crime scene, they've found human fingerprints all over it.

Don't look now, but there are dozens of satellites zooming overhead, observing Earth from space. The Earth Observing System (EOS) isn't watching humans (so you can keep talking to yourself); these satellites are packed with tools to measure Earth's temperature and dozens of scientific factors that affect the climate. Collecting data about what Earth was like in the past is harder, but it's still possible. The thick ice covering Antarctica and Greenland formed over millions of years and is filled with tiny trapped bubbles of ancient air. By drilling ice cores (long cylinders of ice) out of these ice sheets, scientists can test the trapped bubbles to figure out what the atmosphere was like long before humans were around to complain about the weather.

The oldest Antarctic ice cores are almost 2 miles deep and date back 800,000 years. Comparing today's air with the ancient air found in ice cores proves that the mixture of gases in Earth's atmosphere has changed. There is more carbon dioxide, methane, and nitrous oxide in the atmosphere than at any time since humans appeared on the planet.

Where did these extra greenhouse gases come from? Well, we know that carbon dioxide, methane, and nitrous oxide are released by some processes humans have created to make themselves at home. Since the Industrial Revolution began about 200 years ago, humans have been burning vast amounts of fossil fuels (such as coal and oil) to power transportation, industry, heating, and electricity. When we burn these fuels, we release the carbon trapped inside them as carbon dioxide gas. We've also released greenhouse gases by burning forests and replacing them with gigantic farms.

Between 1750 and 2018, the concentration of carbon dioxide in the atmosphere rose by 46 percent due to human activity.

The evidence tells us that **HUMANS** are almost certainly the culprits in climate change. By releasing extra greenhouse gases into the atmosphere, we have increased the planet's natural greenhouse effect, warming Earth. And greenhouse gas emissions continue to rise. A record 37.1 billion tons of carbon dioxide were released into the atmosphere in 2018. That's more than 18 times the mass of all the animals on the planet (including all the humans).

If we do nothing, global warming, climate change, and their effects are almost certain to get worse. Use the facts to explain that we've all helped cause the problem—so we all share responsibility for tackling it.

Time to GET SERIOUS

# DENY THE DENIERS

A surprising number of people deny that climate change is happening. You can help by answering these statements with **SOLID SCIENCE**.

**PLANET-O-METER**

The evidence for global warming is overwhelming—it's hard to argue with a massive melting ice sheet. However, people disagree about **HOW MUCH** the climate will continue to change in the future and the extent to which humans are to blame. Yet there are still people who don't believe in climate change or who deny that it's a problem. Not everyone takes the time to learn about the causes and effects of climate change. Luckily, you can use these solid, science-based answers to set them straight!

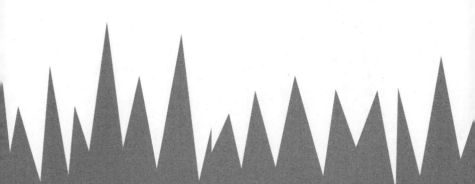

## "IT'S REALLY COLD TODAY. GLOBAL WARMING CAN'T BE TRUE!"

**WEATHER** and **CLIMATE** are different things. *Weather* is what you see when you look out the window on a particular day. *Climate* is the pattern of weather over a **MUCH** longer time period. To help someone understand this, compare it to measuring other things, like how children travel to school. If you glanced out the window only once, you might pick a rainy day and conclude that all children stomp grumpily to school under umbrellas. To find a real answer, you would need to collect data from lots of children over a long time, and spot any patterns. Then you'd need to compare the patterns to data from previous years to find out if anything has really changed. It's the same with weather versus climate change.

**"I LIKE WARM WEATHER—GLOBAL WARMING SOUNDS GREAT TO ME!"**

Spending more time in shorts and less time in sweaters might sound ideal, but remember that the 2°F temperature increase is just a global average. In some places, temperatures have risen far more. And it's not just average temperatures that change. There may be a few places where climate change will bring benefits (such as being able to grow heat-loving crops in places that once were colder). But overall, the bad effects outweigh the good effects everywhere. Melting ice at the poles can lead to flooding thousands of miles away. Extreme weather events, such as droughts in the tropics, can cause food shortages around the world. And climate change doesn't affect only humans; the United Nations predicts that a million animals are already at risk. We all live in the same greenhouse, and climate change is a problem for **EVERYONE**, animals and humans alike, all around the globe.

# EAT YOUR NEIGHBORS

"Food miles" have been popping up in school textbooks for years. Should we ban bananas and other foods that are grown far away?

## PLANET-O-METER

Food miles measure the distance food travels before it ends up on your plate. The concept was first used to highlight that flying or shipping food from elsewhere in the world contributes to climate change, and that eating locally grown food is better. For example, chocolate has a huge carbon footprint—contributing 2.1 **MILLION** tons of greenhouse gases to the atmosphere every year—partly because cocoa from West Africa and the Americas has to be transported to chocolate makers around the world.

Eating a chocolate bar once a week emits
0.2 pounds of carbon dioxide in a year—the same
as driving 205 miles in a gasoline-powered car.

But food miles aren't as simple as they sound. For many foods—including lamb, beef, pork, cheese, canned tuna, eggs, tofu, rice, and nuts—most greenhouse gas emissions happen **LONG** before the food leaves the farm. If local farms can produce a certain food only by using lots of chemicals (because the soil is not good enough), heated polytunnels (because the climate is not warm enough), gallons of water (because the climate is too dry), or lots of heavy machinery, buying that food locally may lead to **GREATER** greenhouse gas emissions than growing it somewhere else and transporting it.

At certain times of year, tomatoes grown in South America are responsible for less carbon dioxide than tomatoes grown out of season in greenhouses in the United States. Even chocolate turns out to be complicated—one study found that 60 percent of the emissions for milk chocolate made in the United Kingdom is due to the locally produced milk, not the cocoa.

So what can you do? Scientists at Harvard University recommend that we eat locally in **TIME** as well as space. Replacing food miles with food space-time?! It sounds like something we might need Einstein to explain, but it's actually pretty simple. It means eating local foods when they are in season—at the time of year when they are ready to harvest in your area. This is when the farming methods and storage are more likely to be eco-friendly. What foods are in season depends on where you live, so you could start with a bit of detective work by searching online. Collect pictures of foods and stick them on a calendar in the kitchen to remind your family which foods are in season that month. You'll also discover that some foods are **NEVER** in season in your area, so you could try to avoid those altogether.

# TURN GARBAGE INTO GROCERIES

You can't get more local than food from your own garden, balcony, or windowsill. Even better, you can grow food from things you'd normally throw away.

**PLANET-O-METER**

Learn to grow new plants from old scraps, and enjoy free food that's good for the planet! Start each project on a sunny windowsill, reusing food packaging as pots (even old egg cartons will work). Potting soil is great for getting them started—you won't need much. Keep them well watered, but don't flood them. When the seedlings look sturdy, transfer them to the garden, or to bigger pots on the windowsill.

## IMMORTAL CARROTS

* Line a saucer with wet cotton pads.
* Press a carrot (or turnip or parsnip) top into the cotton.
* Keep the cotton pads wet.
* Once the tops sprout, plant them in soil outdoors (or indoors in a tall container).

## EVERLASTING GARLIC

* Pull off one clove from a garlic bulb.
* Plant it root downward.
* Put it on a sunny windowsill.
* When shoots appear, keep them trimmed.
* The clove will become a new bulb.

## TIMELESS TOMATOES

* Wash and dry some tomato seeds.
* Plant them in pots in spring.
* When the plants are a few inches high, move them outdoors (or move them into slightly bigger pots and keep them on the windowsill if the weather is chilly).

# TINKER TRAINING

Buying less stuff is one of the best ways to cut your carbon emissions. But what if something breaks—surely you have to replace it?

**PLANET-O-METER**

If you picked up a gadget in a store and the box said, **"THIS WILL BREAK DOWN NEXT YEAR,"** you'd probably put it back on the shelf, right? But, incredibly, many of the things we buy really are designed to have a very short life span. This business model even has a name—planned obsolescence. (Try saying that quickly like a tongue twister and **YOU** might break down!) Some products, from light bulbs to toothbrushes to washing machines, are designed to stop working after a certain time, forcing us to replace them. Other products, such as clothes, cars, and cell phones, are upgraded every few months or years. The aim is to make the old models seem clunky or unfashionable so we want to buy a new version.

In 2018, the EU Parliament voted to try to end the planned obsolescence of electronic gadgets. They want manufacturers to make products easier to repair, and to include information on the packaging about how long they will last.

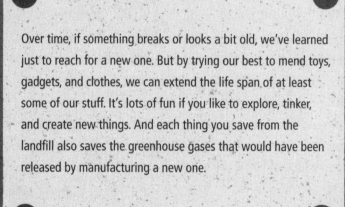

Over time, if something breaks or looks a bit old, we've learned just to reach for a new one. But by trying our best to mend toys, gadgets, and clothes, we can extend the life span of at least some of our stuff. It's lots of fun if you like to explore, tinker, and create new things. And each thing you save from the landfill also saves the greenhouse gases that would have been released by manufacturing a new one.

# COUNTDOWN TO TINKERING SUPERSTARDOM

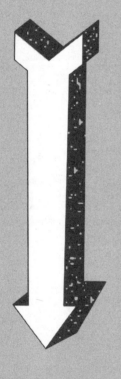

5. Before chucking something that is damaged—whether it's a remote-controlled toy or a pair of jeans—ask an adult to help you search online for a quick guide to repairing it. One site to try is **ifixit.com**.

4. Put your own tinker kit together at home. It could include a sewing kit and spare buttons (see page 76), a screwdriver and screws, a tape measure, pliers, tweezers, strong tape, nontoxic glue, safety pins, crayons, safety goggles, paper clips, rubber bands, scissors, string, and a foam sponge.

3. Get hold of some moldable mending putty, like FORMcard or Sugru. You can use it to repair anything from broken shoes to a loose headphone cord.

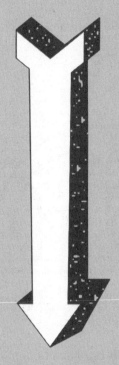

2. If you're really stuck, look for a repair café in your area (visit **repaircafe.org**). These often have tools and materials you can use to fix stuff, as well as volunteers to give you advice or even mend things for you.

1. If you get this far and something **STILL** seems beyond repair, why not "hack" it to make something entirely new from the parts?

In addition to shrinking your carbon footprint, tinkering gives you problem-solving skills that could get you an exciting job in the future. Just ask engineers like Danielle George, Jane ní Dhulchaointigh, or Janese Swanson, who all loved fixing broken stuff as kids.

# START AN ECO-LIBRARY

Libraries are awesome, and they aren't just for books! Imagine a library that lends out toys, costumes, or party gear... then set it up!

**PLANET-O-METER**

Parties and dress-up days are lots of fun, but our special occasions can put pressure on the planet. Costumes, decorations, and party goods are often used just **ONCE** and then thrown away or forgotten. To tackle this problem, communities around the world are setting up lending programs that allow people to rent items for parties and celebrations. Your school is the perfect place to set up a system like this. Here's how.

1 Gather a small team to help you set up your
eco-library, including at least one teacher or
responsible adult volunteer. Decide what you
would like to lend out. Here are some ideas:

✳ Party decorations and reusable tableware
✳ Costumes
✳ Toys and games
✳ Sports equipment

2   Collect your chosen items. The best way is to
     ask families to donate things they no longer use,
     or you could fundraise to buy things from
     thrift stores.

3   Decide on the guidelines for rental. Where can
     families come to borrow items? How many can
     they check out at a time? How long can people
     borrow an item for? Will there be a small fee to
     join the library or borrow items (to fund new
     equipment)? What should families do if they
     accidentally lose or break something? Will they
     need to wash or clean the item before they return
     it? Include all this information when you tell
     school families about the idea.

4   Plan where you will store items between
     rentals. You'll need strong boxes to keep
     them in. Make a list of what's included
     to stick inside the lid of each box. If you
     are lending toys or costumes, include
     information about which age-group or
     size each item is for.

5   Set up a system to record what has been
    borrowed, when, and by whom. This could be a
    simple printed spreadsheet or chart kept in a
    folder. Even if you have only one thing to lend out
    (such as a box of party decorations), you will still
    need a calendar to record reservations.

6   As volunteers, your work is not done yet! Don't
    forget to check items between loans to make sure
    they are clean and safe to lend out again.

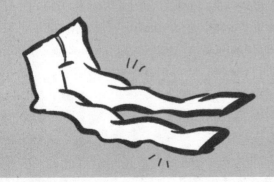

# REWILD YOUR BACKYARD

**Good news—you can fight climate change by doing nothing!**

PLANET-0-METER

A neatly mowed lawn produces very little oxygen and doesn't capture much carbon. But it can be hard to find an area of land that's truly wild. The rewilding movement aims to change that by leaving areas of land to return to a more natural state.

You can scale down the ideas for your own yard or a nearby patch of land. Focus on rewilding plants, and the animals will follow. Just do as little as possible and let your backyard get on with it! If you don't have your own space, ask administrators at your school to let you rewild a patch of playground or playing field. You might not win any best-kept garden prizes, but you'll be helping build a better-kept planet.

# COUNTDOWN TO REWILDING YOUR BACKYARD

5. **STOP** using chemicals. These are often used to control the plants and animals that would naturally live there. Persuade your family to avoid pesticides, weed killers, and artificial fertilizers.

4. **STOP** weeding. You don't need to buy wildflower seeds to get a beautiful wild garden. Just do nothing! So-called weeds will soon find their way to your garden, dropped by animals and carried on the wind. If allowed to grow, these "weeds" will produce beautiful flowers—a great source of food for insects.

3. **STOP** tidying up. Let leaves, twigs, and logs pile up too—they provide hiding places for bugs and other wildlife. The more insects that live in your garden, the more likely it is that larger animals will visit.

2. **STOP** mowing the grass. Wildlife hates a neatly trimmed lawn—nowhere to hide, no flowers to feast on. Leave at least one patch of grass to grow long and wild, and don't cut the rest too short.

1. **MAKE** a pond. Okay, this takes a few minutes of effort, but it's worth it to turn your yard into an exciting safari destination! Reuse an old plastic basin as a pond lining by sinking it into the soil. (Choose a spot with some shade and some sun.) Pop in a few simple pond plants to keep the water fresh and clean. (Leave them in the pots they come in.) Then fill the basin with collected rainwater and wait. It won't be long before wildlife starts moving in.

# BE MORE GRETA

Teenage climate activist Greta Thunberg is single-handedly waking up the world to the climate emergency. There are five simple things we can all do to be more Greta.

PLANET-O-METER

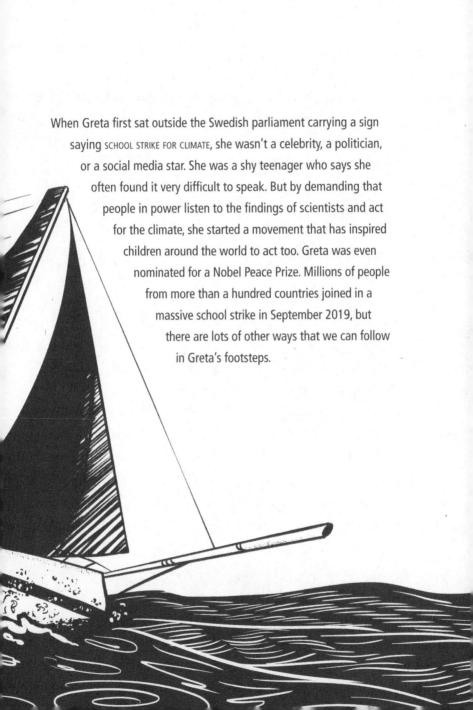

When Greta first sat outside the Swedish parliament carrying a sign saying SCHOOL STRIKE FOR CLIMATE, she wasn't a celebrity, a politician, or a social media star. She was a shy teenager who says she often found it very difficult to speak. But by demanding that people in power listen to the findings of scientists and act for the climate, she started a movement that has inspired children around the world to act too. Greta was even nominated for a Nobel Peace Prize. Millions of people from more than a hundred countries joined in a massive school strike in September 2019, but there are lots of other ways that we can follow in Greta's footsteps.

1   **Do something**—no matter how small. The scale of the climate emergency can seem overwhelming, but Greta's message is that "the one thing we need more than hope is action." Taking positive action helped Greta turn her feelings of sadness about climate change into a feeling that she could do something about it. The ideas in this book will get you started.

2   **Be inspired by others.** Greta's first school strike was inspired by students in Florida, who left class to protest the harm caused by US gun laws.

3   **Take the train.** No matter how important the event, or how long it takes to get there, Greta is determined to avoid fossil fuel–guzzling flights. Instead of flying, she journeys throughout Europe by train or electric car. She even traveled by sailboat across the Atlantic to attend a United Nations global warming summit in New York City!

**<u>4</u>** **Spread the word.** Greta believes that most people would happily help tackle the climate emergency if they knew enough about it. Once Greta learned what the science said, she began spreading the word at home, persuading her father to become vegetarian and her mother to give up flying. Now she focuses on spreading the word to people in power.

**<u>5</u>** **Start now.** You're never too young to take action of some kind. Greta was 9 when she began reading about the climate crisis, 11 when she decided to do something about it, and 15 when she protested outside the Swedish parliament for the first time. There are thousands of ways to take action, and you don't have to do it alone—find out what's happening near you and how you can join in.

# STAY OUT OF HOT WATER

To cut greenhouse gas emissions, we need to burn fewer fossil fuels. Start at home by staying out of hot water.

**PLANET-O-METER**

Unless you happen to live near a hot spring, heating water is likely to be the biggest part of your carbon footprint at home. Some homes have boilers that burn natural gas or oil, roaring to life like boring rectangular dragons and belching out carbon dioxide, methane, and nitrous oxide. Other homes use electricity to heat water. Electric heaters don't produce greenhouse gases directly, but most of the world's electricity is still produced by burning fossil fuels. In Australian households, electric water heaters produce up to **THREE TIMES** as much greenhouse gas as low-emission, fossil fuel–burning heaters. Until more of our power is produced from renewable energy sources, using electricity to heat water is **BAD NEWS**.

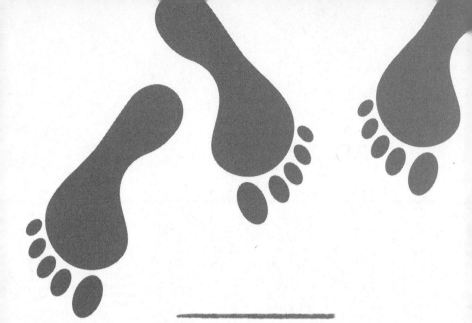

Heating water counts for about 42 percent
of New York City's total greenhouse
gas emissions.

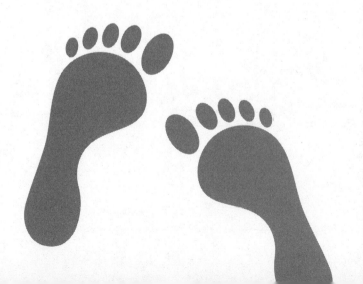

# 5 TIPS FOR STAYING OUT OF HOT WATER AT HOME

1. Using a dishwasher can be more eco-friendly than washing dishes by hand, as long as you run the dishwasher only when full. If you have to wash by hand, keep the water cool and never rinse under a running hot tap.

2. Take showers instead of baths, but remember to keep them short. Spending more than four minutes in a fast-flowing shower can use up far more hot water than a bath does.

3. Wear clothes longer between washes. This eco-tip will help the clothing last longer too. Unless something is noticeably dirty or smelly, keep it out of the laundry.

4. Are you tech-savvy? Do people always call on you to get the computer working? Teach yourself how to program the boiler, too, so it heats water only when your family needs it.

5. If the water from your hot tap is always too hot to use, ask an adult to lower the water temperature on the boiler, water heater, or storage tank. For most homes, 140°F is hot enough.

# TURN THE TAP OFF!

If you're finding it hard to persuade your family that you can save the planet by not washing your gym clothes, remind them that all these tips will save your household money too. In the United States, water heating accounts for about 12 percent of a family's utility bills. Lowering the temperature on your water heater by 10°F could save your family up to 5 percent on water-heating costs.

# SAY NAY TO THE SPRAY

We often use aerosol sprays to make ourselves look and smell good, but for the planet, spraying stinks.

**PLANET-O-METER**

For products like hair spray and deodorants and spray paints, aerosol cans quickly and easily get liquids (and your hair!) in the right place. Before 1987, gases called chlorofluorocarbons (CFCs) were used as the propellants—the gas that escapes when you press the button, forcing some of the liquid out with it. CFCs appeared to be perfect— nontoxic and nonflammable—so it seemed like a nonproblem when they just drifted off into the air.

Then, about 50 years ago, scientists realized with **HORROR** that all the CFCs being released into the air were drifting high into the upper atmosphere, where they messed with a gas called ozone. Ozone is a natural greenhouse gas, but it's also a vital sunscreen that blocks the sun's harmful radiation and makes life on our planet possible. The damage caused by CFCs had created a huge hole in the ozone layer over Antarctica. The problem was so bad that the world's countries quickly agreed to stop using CFCs and similar chemicals.

The Montreal Protocol of 1987 became the most successful international agreement **EVER**, proving that countries can work together to stop environmental damage if they try. By the mid-1990s, the hole in the ozone layer had stopped getting bigger. Scientists are hopeful that it will repair itself by around 2070.

The ban on CFCs was good news for the climate, too, because CFCs are powerful greenhouse gases. However, spray cans are still on our shelves, and the hydrofluorocarbon (HFC) propellants used instead of CFCs are also greenhouse gases. One of them, with the deceptively boring name HFC-134a, is actually a supervillain 1,430 times better at

trapping the sun's heat than carbon dioxide is! Each puff released from a spray can will hang around in the atmosphere for hundreds of years.

The countries that signed the Montreal Protocol have come up with a new agreement—the Kigali Amendment, which challenges countries to phase out HFCs. It would be a small change with a **BIG** impact, preventing up to 0.9°F of future warming. Some countries have risen to the challenge already. Others will follow starting in 2024.

However, not every country has signed on to the Kigali Amendment yet. You can help in two ways. Write to your local politicians to ask them to take action to ratify the Kigali Amendment. Most importantly, avoid using aerosols yourself. Almost anything that comes in an aerosol **CAN** be delivered in other ways—sprays are only popular because they are easy to use.

# TAKE A STAYCATION

Going on vacation can balloon the size of your carbon footprint. Give the planet a break by swapping your next family break for a staycation.

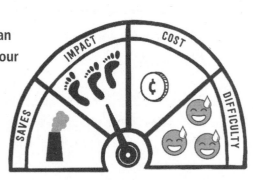

**PLANET-O-METER**

You've probably heard that air travel is bad for the planet, but did you know that a round-trip flight from London to Rome has a larger carbon footprint than the average person in Madagascar or Ethiopia has over an entire **YEAR**?! Swapping a vacation abroad for a "staycation" at home is a terrific way to make a difference and can be super fun too. Ban homework, cooking, and cleaning and dip into this list of adventures.

# 10 TIPS FOR A
# SUPER STAYCATION

1   See how far you can get by public transportation (trains, buses, boats, or streetcars) in just one day.

2   Spend a night sleeping under the stars. In your backyard or at a local campsite, make a shelter you can sleep in, build a campfire, and ask an adult to download a stargazing app.

3   Using an online map, plan a walk (or bike ride), and challenge your whole family to follow the route.

4   Do a tasting tour of your town or city, visiting local food vendors on foot and buying one thing at each to create the ultimate picnic. Then find a park to eat your feast in.

5   Fill a jar with ideas about things to do (set a budget first), and pull them out one at a time during your staycation.

6   Try a new sport locally, such as paddleboarding, paintballing, or visiting a BMX track.

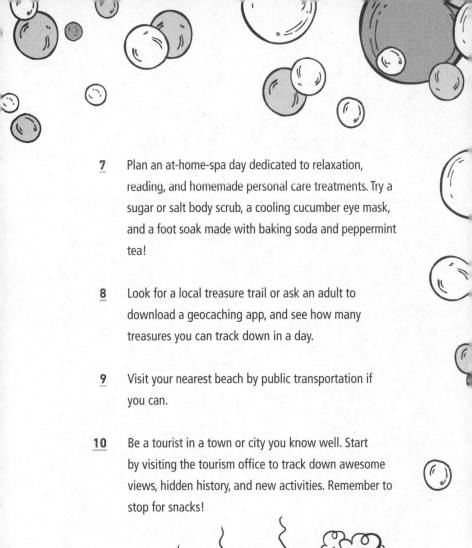

7   Plan an at-home-spa day dedicated to relaxation, reading, and homemade personal care treatments. Try a sugar or salt body scrub, a cooling cucumber eye mask, and a foot soak made with baking soda and peppermint tea!

8   Look for a local treasure trail or ask an adult to download a geocaching app, and see how many treasures you can track down in a day.

9   Visit your nearest beach by public transportation if you can.

10   Be a tourist in a town or city you know well. Start by visiting the tourism office to track down awesome views, hidden history, and new activities. Remember to stop for snacks!

# MEASURE YOUR FEET

When it comes to caring for our planet, we've seriously put our foot in it. Measuring your carbon footprint will help you figure out how YOU contribute to climate change— and what you can do about it.

## PLANET-0-METER

Your carbon footprint tells you roughly how many tons of greenhouse gases are emitted every year as a result of the things you do. It includes greenhouse gases released by burning fossil fuel at home— for example, if your home has a boiler that burns natural gas or oil. It also includes emissions that happen far from your home, such as the greenhouse gases released by power stations that produce the electricity you use, by factories that make the stuff you buy, and by farms that produce the food you eat. In fact, almost everything you use to do the things you do releases greenhouse gases at some point.

This doesn't mean you have to limit yourself to a life of long walks and sitting in the dark (though both are carbon-neutral!). Some of our activities lead to far more greenhouse gas emissions than others. Calculating your carbon footprint is a great way to figure out which changes you can make to have the most **IMPACT**.

Start with some detective work. Gather as much information as possible about the things you and your family do that use energy. If you find information for your whole household—such as the amount of electricity used each year—divide it by the number of people in your household to get a rough figure for just you.

**THEN PLUG THE DATA INTO ONE OF THESE CARBON CALCULATORS, WHICH WILL DO THE MATH FOR YOU!**

CARBONFOOTPRINT.COM/CALCULATOR.ASPX

EPA.GOV/CARBON-FOOTPRINT-CALCULATOR

Once you've calculated your carbon footprint, compare it with the average for the country you live in and for other areas of the world (measured in tons).

QATAR 30.4

AUSTRALIA 15.6

CANADA 15

USA 14.6

SOUTH KOREA 11.7

RUSSIA 10.6

GERMANY 8.7

CHINA 6.7

NORWAY 6.6

UK 5.4

ITALY 5.3

PORTUGAL 4.9

SWEDEN 3.8    UKRAINE 3.8

INDIA 1.6

ETHIOPIA 0.1

# DON'T FEED YOUR TRASH CAN

Food has an enormous (and very stinky) carbon footprint. But you can start to shrink it without giving anything up.

**PLANET-O-METER**

It's not just burning fossil fuels that contributes to global warming. Cutting down trees and raising cattle have an impact too. Add up the greenhouse gas emissions from clearing and farming land and processing, packaging, storing, and transporting food to stores and homes, and you find that feeding the world's 7.7 billion people is responsible for a terrifying **25 PERCENT** of all greenhouse gas emissions. That doesn't even include the energy used to cook the food.

But don't despair! It's possible to shrink your carbon foodprint without giving up a thing. Instead of cutting down on what you eat, cut down on what you **WASTE**.

Food waste is a big problem. About one-third of the food produced in the world each year never gets eaten. This means a third of the greenhouse gas emissions that stem from food production are contributing to global warming for **NO REASON AT ALL**.

The picture below shows how much of each food is wasted every year around the world.

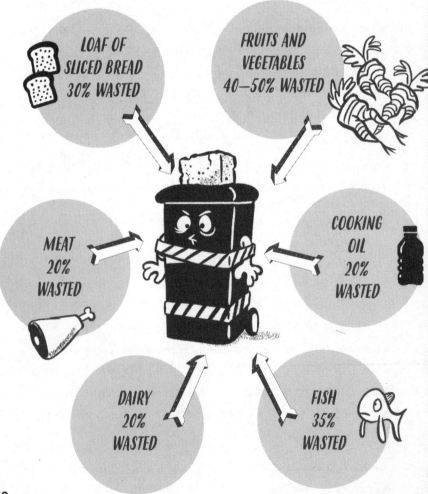

LOAF OF
SLICED BREAD
30% WASTED

FRUITS AND
VEGETABLES
40–50% WASTED

MEAT
20%
WASTED

COOKING
OIL
20%
WASTED

DAIRY
20%
WASTED

FISH
35%
WASTED

# COUNTDOWN
# TO TACKLING
# FOOD WASTE

3. **HELP YOURSELF.** Instead of being given full plates of food at mealtimes, ask your family if everyone could help themselves, taking only as much as they want to eat. This makes it easier to refrigerate or freeze leftovers for another meal.

2. **GET CREATIVE.** Once a week, challenge yourself to cook a meal or prepare a snack using only leftovers and pantry supplies. Find some inspiration online at **bbcgoodfood.com/howto/guide /love-your-leftovers-how-use-surplus -ingredients** and **lovefoodhatewaste .com/recipes**.

1. **KEEP A DIARY.** Whenever someone puts fresh food in the fridge, make a note of the use-by date. If you haven't eaten it by then, freeze it! This even works with milk and cheese. Cut it into cubes first. (The cheese, not the milk. Cubing milk would be an udder failure.)

# PROCRASTINATE FOR THE PLANET

As people earn more money, their carbon footprint increases too. Try this trick to stop your pocket money from burning a hole in the planet.

**PLANET-O-METER**

Even within the same region or neighborhood, individual carbon footprints vary hugely. In some parts of the European Union, for example, individual carbon footprints vary from 0.6 tons to 6.5 tons. What are the reasons for this massive difference? Do people with a small carbon footprint live in special energy-efficient homes? Does their electricity come from solar power? No. Scientists discovered that the only important difference is in income.

# The more money people earn, the bigger their carbon footprint is.

In the European Union, for each extra €1,000 a person earns per year, their emissions increase by 584 pounds.

It's easy to see how it happens. The more money people have, the more stuff they buy (particularly things like clothes and manufactured products) and the higher their emissions. So how can you stop your birthday money or pocket money from burning a hole in your eco efforts? Try this simple trick.

Each time you want to buy something, from a new pair of sneakers to a downloaded game, **WAIT A WEEK** before you make the final decision. A lot of the time, you'll find that the urge to buy fades, and your procrastination will help the planet. (Plus, you'll have more savings for when you **REALLY** need something.)

# GROW A FREE TREE!

Plant-saving, carbon-capturing solutions don't just grow on trees . . . or do they?

PLANET-O-METER

Although we need to cut greenhouse gas emissions, we don't have to reduce them to zero. Instead we need to aim for net zero. This means that any carbon dioxide released **INTO** the atmosphere is canceled out by taking the same amount of carbon dioxide **OUT** of the atmosphere. So, how do we go about capturing something we can't see or touch? The 2015 Paris Climate Agreement talks about "removal by sinks." These aren't the kind of sink you find in your kitchen. They include oceans, lakes, and ponds, which naturally absorb carbon dioxide from the air. They also include the world's forests. Like all plants, trees capture carbon dioxide from the air and save it to make food for later, locking it away in their stems, roots, and leaves—sometimes for thousands of years. So could we solve the world's climate emergency by planting more trees?

Scientists have done the math and figured out that the planet could probably support almost 2.5 **BILLION** acres of extra forest. These additional 500 billion trees would store more than 200 gigatons of extra carbon once fully grown, reducing carbon dioxide in the atmosphere by about 25 percent.

Every tree helps—it doesn't matter if it's in the Amazon rain forest or in your school playground. By channeling our inner gardener and learning to take cuttings from trees that are already grown, we can all plant a tree for free and begin to balance our own carbon emissions.

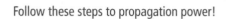

Follow these steps to propagation power!

1  Find a native deciduous tree (or a climbing plant
   or shrub). Get permission from the owner to take
   a cutting.

2  Wait until the tree has just lost its leaves, or just
   before it grows new buds.

3  Find a bit of branch that has grown recently—it
   might be smoother than the rest of the branch or
   a different color. Cut off the soft tip.

4  Cut a section of branch slightly shorter than
   a classroom ruler, cutting just above a bud.

5  Dip that end in a rooting powder—this contains
   nutrients that will make the cutting grow roots!

6  Choose a sheltered place (or a pot). Add some
   compost to the soil to give your cutting a good start.

7  Push the cutting into the ground or a pot so that
   two-thirds is hidden below the surface.

8  Leave the cutting alone. Collect rainwater to keep
   it hydrated in summer. It may not do much for a
   year—all the action is happening underground.

# STOP RECYCLING...

... unless it's a last resort! Always focus on reducing and reusing first.

## PLANET-O-METER

Many people have heard the mantra "reduce, reuse, recycle," but the last R always hogs the spotlight. It even has its own logo. Since the 1980s, recycling has been seen as a solution to all sorts of problems, from overcrowded landfills to plastic pollution. But the reality of recycling doesn't live up to its reputation. Each time we toss something into the recycling bin, we're not being as green as we think we are.

**PLASTIC IS THE PERFECT EXAMPLE.** It's not just a leading source of pollution. Plastic has a massive carbon footprint, too. It requires energy to produce, form into products, and transport to stores. At the moment, most of this energy comes from burning fossil fuels, releasing greenhouse gases into the atmosphere. Most plastic is also **MADE FROM** a fossil fuel (petroleum oil).

Yet plastic has never been more popular: 322 million tons were produced worldwide in 2015, and in the same year emissions from plastic were responsible for almost 1.8 billion tons of carbon dioxide—more than the entire country of Japan. Demand for plastic is growing so quickly that it will be responsible for 15 percent of global carbon emissions by 2050—that's more than air travel!

**RECYCLING PLASTIC ONLY HELPS A LITTLE.** For starters, collecting, transporting, sorting, and cleaning used plastic—and the recycling process itself—all gobble up energy and other resources. But most plastic doesn't even get this far. Only certain types of plastic can be recycled (or are profitable to recycle). It's usually cheaper and easier to make plastic from scratch, so over 90 percent of plastic goes unrecycled, even if it's put in a recycling bin.

What actually happens to plastic waste in the
United States?

**16%** incinerated
**76%** landfilled
**8%** recycled

At the moment, 1 MILLION TONS of plastic
collected for recycling in the United States each
year is shipped overseas for processing. What's
the point of cutting down on your own travel
only to send your litter on a long-haul voyage?

If recycling can't get us out of this mess, what is the solution?
We need to stop telling ourselves it's okay to grab a single-use plastic
bottle, bag, or straw because we'll recycle it. Instead, we need to
focus on the other two Rs—Reduce and Reuse. Reduce comes first for
a reason. Buying less stuff (see page 62) is the **BEST** way to tackle
climate change **AND** plastic pollution in one go. If you **REALLY** need
to buy something plastic, make sure it is reusable (or buy it
secondhand, so **YOU** do the reusing).

# BEAT THE JARGON

Understanding the science behind climate change is the key to finding solutions. Learn to unlock acronyms and decipher climate-change jargon so you'll always have the science on your side.

## PLANET-O-METER

### ACIDIFICATION

Oceans absorb carbon dioxide from the atmosphere. This can help keep the atmosphere in balance, but it also makes the water more acidic, which is bad for wildlife.

## CARBON CAPTURE

Anything that takes carbon out of the atmosphere and stores it. Carbon sinks do this naturally (see page 65), but people are trying to invent ways to speed up the process. It's sometimes called carbon sequestration.

## CARBON DIOXIDE (CO$_2$)

A gas in Earth's atmosphere that plants need to make food. It's released when plants or fossil fuels are burned. Carbon dioxide is the main greenhouse gas that humans produce.

## CARBON FOOTPRINT

A measure of the impact of something (or someone) on the environment, through the greenhouse gases they are responsible for.

## CARBON-NEUTRAL

Counterbalancing the greenhouse gases produced by certain activities with activities that capture greenhouse gases.

## CARBON OFFSETTING

Action to capture or reduce greenhouse gas emissions (like planting trees) in order to compensate for action that releases greenhouse gases (like air travel).

## CLIMATE

The pattern of weather conditions that is typical for an area over a long time—for example, the average temperature, or the average rainfall, or the average number of sunny days in a typical season or year.

## CLIMATE CHANGE

A pattern of change in the climate of the world or a region of the world.

## DEFORESTATION

The clearing of trees in a wooded area.

## EMISSIONS

Greenhouse gases released into the atmosphere.

## $CO_2e$

Our emissions are made up of different combinations of greenhouse gases. A carbon dioxide equivalent ($CO_2e$) is a measure used to compare the climate effects of the various gases relative to carbon dioxide. This unit describes how much carbon dioxide it would take to cause the same amount of environmental damage as a particular combination of these greenhouse gases.

## FOSSIL FUELS

Coal, oil, and natural gas, which formed from plants and animals over millions of years. They store lots of energy, which is released when they are burned, making them useful fuels. But burning fossil fuels also produces carbon dioxide, a greenhouse gas.

## GLOBAL AVERAGE TEMPERATURE

The average temperature of Earth's surface, measured by averaging thousands of temperature readings from around the world, over long periods of time.

## GLOBAL WARMING

A steady rise in global average temperature over a long time, which scientists say is caused by greenhouse gas emissions from human activities.

## GREENHOUSE EFFECT

A process that occurs when certain gases collect in Earth's atmosphere and trap the sun's heat, warming the planet's surface and lower atmosphere.

## GREENHOUSE GASES

Certain gases in Earth's atmosphere that trap heat and warm Earth's surface.

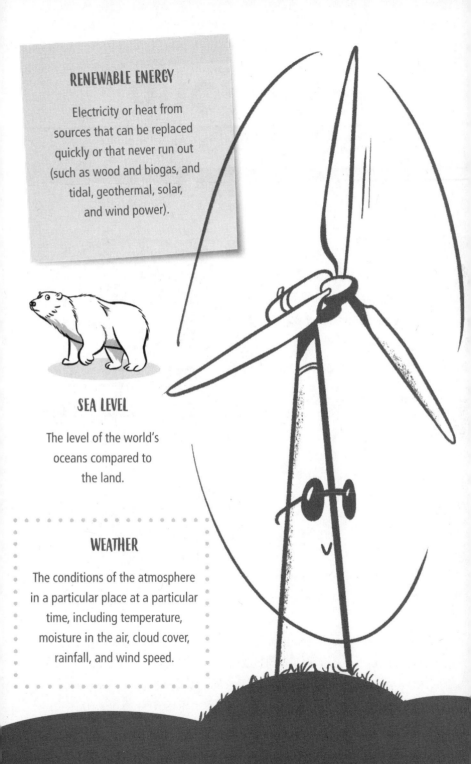

## RENEWABLE ENERGY

Electricity or heat from sources that can be replaced quickly or that never run out (such as wood and biogas, and tidal, geothermal, solar, and wind power).

## SEA LEVEL

The level of the world's oceans compared to the land.

## WEATHER

The conditions of the atmosphere in a particular place at a particular time, including temperature, moisture in the air, cloud cover, rainfall, and wind speed.

# MAKE YOUR CLOTHES IMMORTAL

**What do a T-shirt and a 75-mile road trip have in common?**

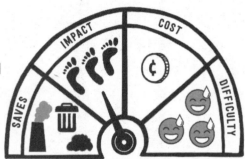

PLANET-O-METER

They are both responsible for about 33 pounds of carbon dioxide emissions. For the T-shirt, just over half of this carbon footprint comes from the energy used for washing, drying, and ironing, assuming it's worn 50 times. This means you could cut your carbon footprint by washing and ironing your clothes less often. You could cut it even further by buying fewer clothes—and making the ones you do have last as long as possible.

On average, we wear a piece of clothing for 2.2 years before getting rid of it. The most common reasons for throwing away clothes are because they don't fit or they are damaged and beyond repair (or we choose not to repair them). But making simple fixes can be easy.

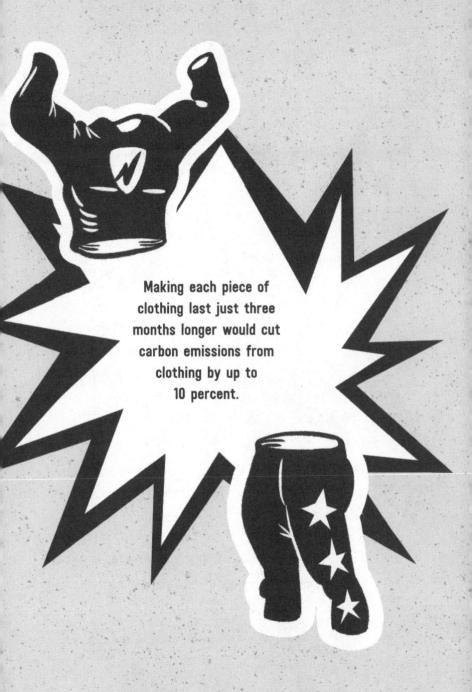

Making each piece of clothing last just three months longer would cut carbon emissions from clothing by up to 10 percent.

## STAIN AWAY

If you have a pesky stain like tomato, mustard, or grass, soak the stained fabric in vinegar, then wash as usual. If the stain is really tough, make a paste by mixing white vinegar and baking soda; rub it into the stain with an old toothbrush before washing as usual. If the stain is really, really stubborn, sew or glue on a patch to camouflage it!

## GET OUT OF A HOLE

If you have a tear or hole in your clothing, find a bit of scrap fabric to pin on the back, then sew back and forth over it, to make the mend strong. No matching thread? No problem! You can treat each mend as an excuse to add a colorful new feature and customize your clothes.

## COMING UNZIPPED

If a zipper is stuck, rub a pencil along the teeth to loosen it. If that doesn't work, try doing the same with a bar of soap or a tube of lip balm. If one of the teeth of the zipper looks wonky, use pliers (see page 30) to bend it back into place. If the problem is a missing zipper pull, replace it with something else, from a paper clip to a fun key ring.

# UPDATE YOUR PLATE

**We can help prevent global warming by eating less meat. Happily, this change has benefits for your health—and your bank account.**

PLANET-O-METER

In addition to gobbling up land, crops, and water, livestock (animals farmed for food) have an enormous carbon footprint. Compare the greenhouse gas emissions released by getting 3.5 ounces of your favorite foods into your home.

**BEEF** 110.2 LB. $CO_2$E

**LAMB** 44.1 LB. $CO_2$E

**CHEESE** 24.3 LB. $CO_2$E

GALLON OF **MILK** 17.6 LB. $CO_2$E

**PORK** 16.7 LB. $CO_2$E

FARMED **FISH** 13.2 LB. $CO_2$E

**CHICKEN** 12.6 LB. $CO_2$E

DARK **CHOCOLATE** 10.1 LB. $CO_2$E

**EGGS** 9.3 LB. $CO_2$E

**GRAINS** 6 LB. $CO_2$E

**LEGUMES** 2 LB. $CO_2$E

**ROOT VEGGIES** 0.9 LB. $CO_2$E

**SUGAR** 0.7 LB. $CO_2$E

Many people love eating meat, and all sorts of cuisines build dishes and meals around it. Meat provides protein, which we need to build, maintain, and repair our bodies. But there are plenty of other good sources of protein, including fish, eggs, and plant-based foods such as beans, lentils, peas, soybeans, and nuts. After all, most of the animals we eat build **THEIR** bodies by eating plants.

---

**Our bodies can't tell the difference between protein from beans and protein from beef. But producing beef uses 20 times as much land and releases 20 times as many greenhouse gases.**

---

Cattle are the real villains in this story. Nearly 60 percent of all the world's farmland is used to raise and feed beef cattle, but this beef provides just 2 percent of the energy in our food. As the world's population continues to grow, that land is desperately needed to grow crops for humans to eat.

To lower your carbon footprint and help save the planet, many experts suggest switching to a plant-based "flexitarian" diet. This means eating vegetarian or vegan meals most of the time, with only small amounts of meat, dairy, and fish.

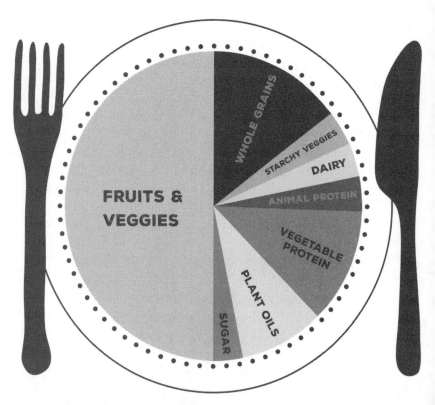

In some countries, eating flexitarian would introduce **MORE** meat at mealtimes, to ensure that everyone has fair access to a healthy diet. In countries like the United States, where people eat **THREE TIMES** as much meat as the global average, a flexitarian diet would mean cutting back.

# COUNTDOWN TO A FLEXITARIAN DIET

5. Begin by giving up meat for just one day a week.

4. On other days, try replacing some of the meat in each meal with beans, grains, or vegetables—for example, by mixing lentils with meat to make burgers.

3. Consider giving up red meat altogether.

2. Learn how to cook vegetarian (meat-free) meals.

1. Going vegan (eating no animal products at all) can dramatically reduce your contribution to climate change. But vegans need to plan their meals carefully to make sure they get all the protein they need.

# TAKE IT FROM A T. REX

Digging up dinosaur bones isn't just for history buffs. The past has plenty to teach us about the present and the future of life on Earth.

**PLANET-O-METER**

Prehistoric fossils aren't only good at attracting crowds to museums. They tell us about past life on Earth—and not just who had the most teeth. We can use fossils to find out when different types of plants and animals lived and when they became extinct. This fossil record tells us that there have been five huge extinction events in Earth's history—strange periods when most of Earth's plant and animal species . . . disappeared. All these mass extinction events occurred at the same time as unusual changes in the environment, a big clue that we should take climate change seriously. The most famous extinction event is the one that marked the end of the dinosaurs. It's thought to have been caused by a mountain-sized meteorite that slammed into Earth, filling the atmosphere with boiled rock and gases, or by giant volcanic eruptions that pumped carbon dioxide into the atmosphere, or both! Yet that wasn't even the most dramatic extinction event. At the end of the Permian period, about 250 million years ago, more than 90 percent of all existing plant and animal species were lost.

Figuring out what caused this mass extinction is tricky. (Permian archosauromorphs were really bad at keeping diaries.) But all the signs point to a spike in greenhouses gases (caused by a giant volcano and methane-burping bacteria), which led to sudden global warming.

Scientists have found evidence that today's **HUMAN**-caused global warming may be contributing to a sixth mass extinction. Animal and plant species are disappearing 100 times faster than the normal rate, and a million species are thought to be at risk of extinction in the next few years. Life on Earth **HAS** recovered from previous extinction events, but this takes millions of years, and the world looks very different afterward. It's something that all species would rather avoid—take it from a T. rex!

# PEE ON THE COMPOST PILE!

**While you're rewilding the backyard, you could try one of the world's oldest natural fertilizers!**

**PLANET-O-METER**

IMPACT

COST

**0**

SAVES

DIFFICULTY

The fertilizers that many farmers and gardeners use are simply collections of nutrients needed by plants—such as nitrogen, phosphates, and potassium. All these chemicals are also found dissolved in our pee! (When we eat food, our body takes only what it needs and pees or poops out the rest.) Scientists in Nepal did an experiment to find out if pee can help crops grow as well as store-bought fertilizer does, and the answer was a resounding **YES**.

A typical adult produces 0.2 to 0.4 gallons of urine every day. Over one year, this would be enough to fertilize 360 to 480 square yards of crops!

When fertilized with compost and human pee, sweet pepper plants grew taller and had more fruit compared with peppers grown using just fertilizer. Similar experiments with cabbage, tomato, cucumber, and pumpkin plants have shown that fruits and veggies fertilized with pee are just as safe to eat. (The cabbage tasted normal too—phew!)

If you want to try this trick in your own garden, follow these three simple rules:

1   Urine needs to be sanitized before you use it on food plants (usually by storing it in a sealed container for a month). If this is tricky to arrange, stick to sprinkling only on plants you won't be eating.

2   The scientists in Nepal found that pee works best when it's mixed with compost. This is exactly what one organization, the National Trust, has been doing in the United Kingdom. So you could occasionally pee straight onto your compost pile!

3   If you are using pee on your flower beds, dilute it with water first. Very diluted pee can be used to water plants up to twice a week. Make sure you pour it on the soil and not on the plants themselves, as pee can be quite alkaline and salty, which can damage plants. Or mix undiluted pee into soil **BEFORE** you plant.

# UNPLUG FOR THE PLANET

We're all drawn to the worlds on our screens, but spending our lives plugged in isn't great for the real world.

PLANET-O-METER

Science has shown that screen time . . . isn't that bad for us. In fact, scientists at the universities of Oxford and Cardiff in the United Kingdom have found that one to two hours per day on our computers, video games, or smartphones may even be good for teenagers' mental well-being. It can help us feel competent and independent. Lots of games involve creative problem-solving and connecting with other people. But the benefits of gaming come with downsides, too. They encourage billions of us to spend far more than one or two hours a day plugged in.

In the United States each year, gaming has the environmental impact of 85 million refrigerators or 5 million cars.

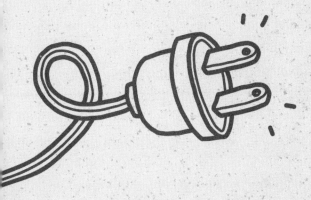

Swapping just an hour of screen time each day for an eco-friendly alternative can make a meaningful difference to your carbon footprint, so here are five things to do in a screen-free hour.

1    You don't need digital blocks to build a new world. Write or draw your way into your imagination.

2    Movies and games absorb us because they make us care about characters. Start reading a new book series for the same feeling.

3    The satisfaction from perfecting a new skill is unbeatable. Teach yourself something that takes a while to master, like a new sport, a musical instrument, or even some challenging magic tricks. With an hour a day, you could be in top form within a year!

4    Do some real-life world building, by creating a small terrarium (indoor garden) or rewilding a bigger outdoor space (see page 36).

5   Round up friends and family and sample a different board game, card game, or word game each week.

# BREAK THE FASHION RULES

Strange as it sounds, fashion is all about making you feel LESS stylish. Break the fashion rules and save the planet at the same time.

## PLANET-O-METER

Fashion gurus are masters at planned obsolescence (see page 27). By introducing new clothing designs every six months (or more often), the old ones quickly fall out of fashion, convincing us that we aren't stylish unless we buy something new. "Fast fashion" is a genius way to get us to spend huge amounts of money on clothes, most of which we don't really need.

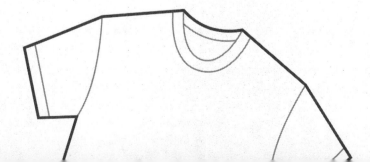

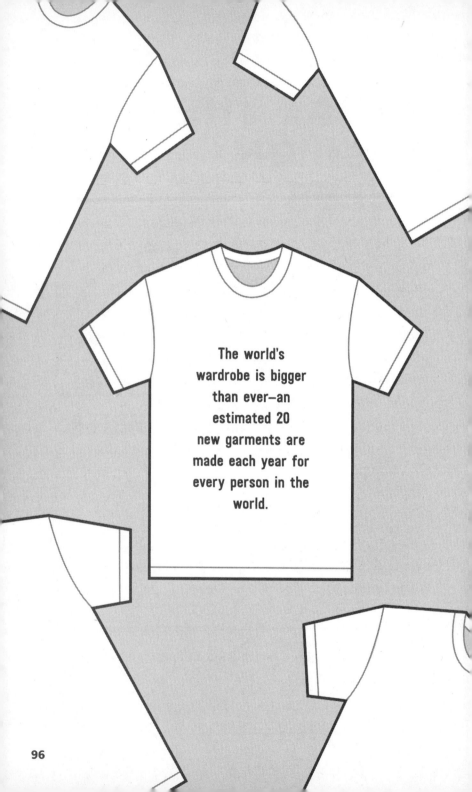

The world's wardrobe is bigger than ever—an estimated 20 new garments are made each year for every person in the world.

Sadly, fast fashion has a shocking cost to the planet, too. Textile production is one of the world's most polluting industries, with a carbon footprint of 1.2 billion tons every year. More than 60 percent of these textiles become clothing. If you look at the labels on your clothes, you'll see that a large number are made in China and India, where much of the power still comes from power plants that burn coal. This boosts the emissions from clothing to 5 to 10 percent of **ALL** global greenhouse gas emissions.

We can encourage our favorite brands to take action by making fast fashion unfashionable. You can start by never throwing old clothes away—sell them, pass them on to another family, or donate them to a charity. And swap mall shopping trips for pre-loved style hunts.

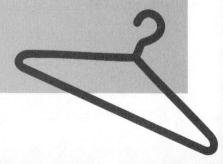

# THREE WAYS TO BUY PRE-LOVED CLOTHES

1   Ask an adult with a smartphone to help you sell and shop using online marketplaces or apps such as Depop, Reshopper, or thredUp. It's easy to search by brand, color, size, and style.

2   Hold a "swishing" party or event at your school, where everyone exchanges clothes they don't like or that don't fit anymore for something "new to you."

3   Don't forget local thrift stores. They get donations all the time, so drop in often for a quick browse. Don't be put off if an item needs a small repair—turn to page 78 to learn how to fix it yourself.

# ASSIGN YOUR SCHOOL SOME HOMEWORK

Schools are part of the problem and can be part of the solution.

PLANET-O-METER

The Australian Youth Climate Coalition is calling for schools to "repower" with clean energy, by installing solar power systems on their roofs. This could reduce emissions by as much as taking 24,500 cars off the road! Not every school gets enough sun to use renewable energy directly or can afford to invest in solar panels, but every school can do something to tackle global warming. Set up a green group at your school (this could involve staff and administrators as well as students), and find out which of the following ideas might work for you.

 *In the United Kingdom, schools are responsible for 2 percent of the country's*

# GREENHOUSE GAS EMISSIONS!

1. **Start a campaign.** Pick one or two ways in which students and staff could become more eco-friendly and start a movement to get everyone on board.  This could include actions like switching off lights and computers, using less paper, or arranging carpools to get to and from school.

2. **Ask to learn about climate change.** Some schools are already building climate change into the curriculum, and one area of northern England plans to train a climate-change teacher in every school. The more you ask, the more likely teachers and school leaders are to sign up for initiatives like this.

3. **Make school trips local.** Rather than taking a tour bus, visit somewhere on foot or by train. Building dens in nearby woods or holding a video conference with an astronaut might be more memorable than taking a trip to a distant museum. Or keep it ultra-local and invite speakers to visit your school.

**4. Take red meat off the menu.**
You could start small with meat-free Mondays, or go the whole heifer and ask your school to ban beef. If you need inspiration, the catering department at the University of Cambridge in the United Kingdom has already stopped serving beef and lamb! See page 80 to find out why this is a good idea, and visit 0beef.com for a Change Pack to help convince your school.

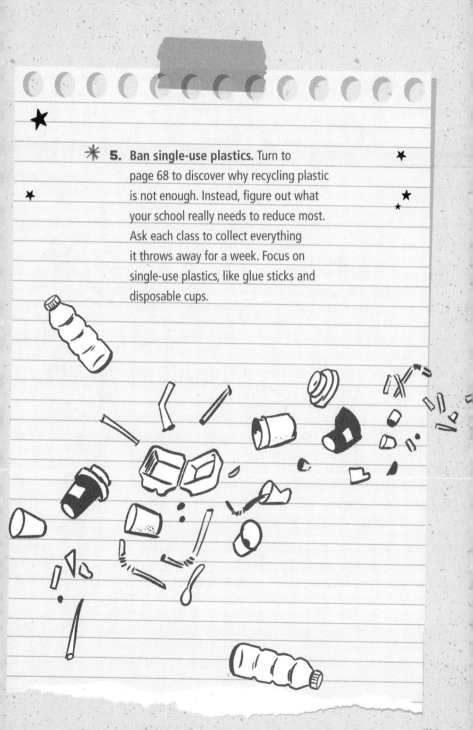

**5. Ban single-use plastics.** Turn to page 68 to discover why recycling plastic is not enough. Instead, figure out what your school really needs to reduce most. Ask each class to collect everything it throws away for a week. Focus on single-use plastics, like glue sticks and disposable cups.

# DON X-RAY SPECS . . .

. . . to see through colorful labels and marketing jargon.

PLANET-0-METER

Believe it or not, food is responsible for almost **ONE-THIRD** of global greenhouse gas emissions. But not all foods deserve an equal share of the blame. Ultra-processed foods are some of the key culprits. These foods have been made using lots of different industrial processes, consuming energy at each stage. The processes change the foods to make them last longer or taste different—often by adding ingredients like salt, oil, and sugar.

It's difficult to visualize the carbon footprint of most processed foods; most of the emissions happen long before you take a bite. But there are clues on the labels that can help you figure out if a food or drink is particularly bad for the planet. Knowing the telltale signs is like having **X-RAY SPECS** that let you see through the colorful packaging.

# 5 CLUES THAT A FOOD MAY BE HEAVILY PROCESSED AND BAD FOR THE PLANET

## 2. IT CONTAINS PALM OIL.

Vast areas of rain forest have been cleared and burned to plant the palm trees that produce this vegetable oil. Deforestation is the second-biggest source of human-caused carbon dioxide emissions, after burning fossil fuels. When land is cleared, fewer trees are left to absorb carbon dioxide from the atmosphere. Palm oil is thought to be in about half of products on supermarket shelves, and dozens of different names are used for it. Look out for these telltale ingredients: palmitate, glyceryl, palm kernel, palmate, palmitic acid, palmitoyl, sodium palm kernelate, sodium lauryl sulfate, stearate, or stearic acid.

## 3. IT CONTAINS HIGH-FRUCTOSE CORN SYRUP.

This sugary syrup is made from corn, using lots of processes and lots of energy. It's often a cheap sweetener in soda, and you might also spot it in breakfast cereals, salad dressings, yogurts, peanut butter, and jam. Using your X-ray specs, look out for the ingredients corn syrup, tapioca syrup, fructose, glucose-fructose syrup, and isoglucose—they're all the same thing.

**1. IT CONTAINS MORE THAN FIVE INGREDIENTS. THIS IS A SIGN THAT IT'S LIKELY TO BE ULTRA-PROCESSED.**

## 4. IT CONTAINS SOY.

Soybeans make their way into 60 percent of processed food in all sorts of ways, including as flour and oil and as a preservative. Soybeans are also used to feed livestock, so we eat soy indirectly through meat and dairy. Nearly half of the world's soy comes from Brazil and Argentina, where huge areas of forest and grassland have been cleared to grow the crop. This releases greenhouse gases into the atmosphere and destroys natural carbon sinks.

## 5. IT'S WHITE, BUT IT COULD BE BROWN.

Bread, pasta, cookies, cakes, noodles, crackers, tortillas, and waffles are all made from grains such as wheat, corn, and rice. They can be made from whole grains (using all parts of the seed) or from refined grains, which have been processed to remove part of the seed. Refined flours are often pale in color, sometimes because they have been bleached. They require more energy and resources to make, so they have a bigger impact on the environment. Choose foods made with whole grains (like brown bread, whole wheat pasta, and brown rice) if possible—they are better for the planet **AND** for your body.

# ASK AWKWARD QUESTIONS

When is buying stuff GOOD for the planet? When you harness your consumer power to demand change!

## PLANET-O-METER

## CLIMATE NEWS

# Just 100 Companies Responsible for 71% of Global Emissions, Scientific Study Says

When you read headlines like the one above, you might feel that you can't do much about the climate emergency unless you happen to be CEO of a major corporation. But remember, all these companies are producing things for **us**. If we stop demanding these goods, companies will stop producing them. So start demanding something different.

One way to do this is to ask questions every time you shop—and make choices based on the answers. This puts pressure on businesses to change, to provide what their customers want. For example, if everyone buying a digital device asked how much electricity it gobbles up while on standby, more companies would start to install power-saving switches.

Was it made using **RENEWABLE ENERGY?**

How **LONG** will it last?

Were the raw materials **ETHICALLY SOURCED?**

Is it **EASY TO MEND** if it breaks?

What is its **CARBON FOOTPRINT?**

What should I do with it when I'm **FINISHED?**

What are your company's **ENVIRONMENTAL POLICIES?**

# DON'T FORGET TO ASK YOURSELF SOME QUESTIONS TOO:

HOW OFTEN WILL I USE IT?

DO I REALLY NEED IT?

COULD I BORROW IT INSTEAD?

# ACT LIKE
# IT'S AN
# EMERGENCY . . .

. . . because it is!
The time to take action
is now, not in the
future. Can you
persuade others
to think this way?

**PLANET-O-METER**

---

**emergency** *(emer-gen-cy)*

*noun*

a serious, unexpected, and often dangerous situation requiring
immediate action

---

Sounds like climate change, right? But at the moment, few people are acting like it's an emergency. We know what we **SHOULD** be doing to tackle global warming, but it's easy to put it off until the future— perhaps because we look around and see other people doing nothing, or because **JUST ONE** car trip won't make a difference.

The problem is, 7.7 **BILLION** people are thinking the same thing.

In 2019, members of the UK Parliament became the first in the world to declare a national climate emergency, inspired by young climate campaigners such as Greta Thunberg and the student strikers. They called on the government to take urgent and ambitious steps, just as they would for any emergency. Other local, state, and national governments are following in their footsteps.

## WHAT CAN YOU DO?

1   Find out if your local, state, or national government has officially declared a climate emergency. If not, contact your local representatives and ask them why not (see page 157).

2   Sign (or start) a petition calling on leaders to declare a climate emergency.

3   Set up a booth at the playground to share information about declaring a climate emergency with as many people as possible.

Will it actually make a difference? After all, "emergency" is just a word, and it doesn't come with a set of rules for dealing with climate change. Many people think it will. Declaring a climate emergency puts pressure on people in power to act quickly and to put climate action at the top of every agenda. Language can be powerful—if people hear "climate crisis" instead of "climate change," "dangerous" instead of "polluting," and "safe" instead of "green," they might listen more closely and be more likely to take positive action.

After all, it *is* an emergency. The United Nations has reported that one climate-related disaster happens every week, costing an estimated $520 billion of damage every year. In Greenland, melting sea ice as a result of global warming is changing people's way of life, which affects their mental health. In India, temperatures surging over 122°F have caused drought, leaving tens of thousands of villages without drinking water. It's not fair to wait until the climate crisis starts affecting you personally. Global warming is a global problem with global causes. Solving it needs to be at the top of **EVERYONE'S** to-do list.

TIME TO ACT

# DON'T GET TOO DRAINED

What's the connection between a Mars rover, a remote-controlled helicopter, and your Candy Crush score?

**PLANET-O-METER**

SAVES · IMPACT · COST · DIFFICULTY

They're all powered by lithium-ion batteries! Better batteries might be a big part of a carbon-neutral future. These are already used in electric cars, but giant batteries may one day store electricity generated from renewable sources, like wind and solar power.

However, producing, using, and safely disposing of lithium-ion batteries gobbles up so much energy, water, and other resources that some electric cars are currently responsible for more greenhouse gas emissions than are gas- and diesel-fueled cars.

You probably don't have your own electric car yet, but taking care of the small lithium-ion batteries that power toys and digital devices can reduce waste and help counter climate change too.

# COUNTDOWN TO BEING A GOOD BATTERY OWNER

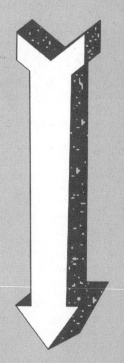

5. **Keep them cool.** Overheating damages lithium-ion batteries, causing them to stop working sooner. Try to keep devices below 86°F. Avoid leaving them in hot places, like on a sunny windowsill or in a car on a sunny day. Take the cover off before charging it, and put the device somewhere heat can escape easily (not shoved down the back of a sofa). And use fast chargers for only a few minutes at a time—they cause batteries to heat up more.

4. **Avoid extremes.** Charging lithium-ion batteries to 100 percent and then using them until they reach zero ages them much faster. This is because they have to work harder when the charge is low. Do small, regular charges that keep the battery between 30 percent and 80 percent all the time.

3. **Be less demanding.** Lithium-ion batteries in consumer products only last for 300 to 500 charge-discharge cycles until they die. Extend their life by closing all apps you're not using, so nothing is running in the background, and turning off Wi-Fi when you know you can't get a signal.

2. **Take charge naps.** Recharging batteries overnight can be a good way to use electricity when demand is lower, but keeping them plugged in once they're fully charged can damage them. If you have a timer plug, use it to stop charging your device after an hour or so.

1. **Avoid parasites.** Using your device as you charge the battery is known as parasitic load. It's fine to check messages, but streaming a video or playing a game while charging is bad for your battery. Try to turn off your device while charging.

# INVITE AN EXPERT

A visit from a local expert on climate change can help you understand the problems and inspire you to take action in new ways.

## PLANET-O-METER

Ask an adult to help you find out if there are any experts in your area. Your teacher could also invite people to do a Skype visit. Turn the page for some ideas for the types of experts you could try.

# EXPERTS TO INVITE TO YOUR SCHOOL

* SCIENTISTS AT NEARBY UNIVERSITIES WHO ARE RESEARCHING CLIMATE, ENVIRONMENT, OR GREEN POLICY

* CLIMATE CHANGE ORGANIZATIONS OR BUSINESSES

* NATURE AND WILDLIFE GROUPS

* A LOCAL PARK RANGER

* THE HEAD OF A LOCAL GREEN GROUP OR REPAIR CAFÉ

* TEENAGERS INVOLVED IN CLIMATE ACTIVISM

* PEOPLE WHO WORK FOR ORGANIZATIONS SUCH AS GREENPEACE

* ARTISTS OR MUSICIANS WHO ARE INSPIRED BY THE ENVIRONMENT

* JOURNALISTS OR AUTHORS WHO WRITE ABOUT CLIMATE CHANGE (HINT, HINT)

# THEN PLAN WHAT TO DO DURING THE VISIT

✳ INVITE THEM TO GIVE AN ASSEMBLY OR CLASS TALK.

✳ GIVE THEM A TOUR OF YOUR SCHOOL, SHOW THEM WHAT YOU ARE ALREADY DOING, AND ASK FOR THEIR IDEAS.

✳ ENCOURAGE THEM TO HELP WITH OR LAUNCH A CAMPAIGN.

✳ LET YOUR SCHOOL PAPER OR STUDENT COUNCIL INTERVIEW THEM AND SHARE THEIR RECOMMENDATIONS.

✳ RECORD A PODCAST TO SHARE ON YOUR SCHOOL WEBSITE.

Once you've put the expert's advice into action, remember to send regular updates, and inspire others to follow in their footsteps.

# AVOID FOUR WHEELS

Cars are wheel-y bad news for the environment, but can you do anything about it if you can't even drive?

**PLANET-O-METER**

**YES!** Start by keeping a travel diary for about a month. Track every car trip where you were a passenger and the trip was (mainly) about getting YOU from place to place—for example, to and from school, after-school activities, a friend's house, or a party. Zoom to page 150 to read about alternatives to driving to school, but skid to a stop on this page for ideas about reducing the carbon footprint of other trips.

1   Start by highlighting short journeys where you could have walked, biked, or scooted. Write down what stopped you, and come up with some ideas for overcoming those obstacles.

2   You'll be more likely to use foot or pedal power if you feel comfortable and safe. Make sure your bike or scooter is in good condition—a bike shop or repair café may be able to check for you. Wear a helmet and layers of clothing that you can take off and put on if the weather changes. There are plenty of apps and websites that will help you plan a safe route, such as bikemap.net and adventurecycling.org.

3   Walking, scooting, and cycling can mean that you need to allow longer for a trip (though not always—one report found that drivers in New York City each spend 107 hours a year looking for parking spaces).

If you're planning a longer hike, use a map and see if you can explore a park, a playground, or an unfamiliar area on the way that you wouldn't see if you were stuck in a car.

**4** For longer journeys, book in advance for cheaper bus and train fares. See if you can purchase tickets with a family or young person's discount. They can save you **TONS** of money. For example, if you go on vacation in Europe, two children ages 4 to 11 can travel **FREE** in 31 countries with an adult who has a Eurail pass!

**5** For those trips where you have to travel by car (such as a birthday party miles from a train station or bus stop), try to share rides whenever possible. It's better if one full car makes the journey than two half-empty cars. You can help to organize the carpool—it's more fun to travel with friends!

# CAST YOUR VOTE

A local or national election is a great time to tell the world what's important to YOU. Hold a mock election at school to bring climate issues into focus.

**PLANET-O-METER**

If there's an election on the horizon, your local candidates will be eager to speak to as many people as possible. Invite them to your school to talk about climate change. After the candidate visits, hold a mock vote. If it's not possible for candidates to visit, hold a shadow election with pupils representing each party and its policies.

1 **Send invitations.** The best way is to email the candidates or their offices (ask a teacher to help). Tell them your school is a part of their electorate (the people who vote them into their jobs) and you would like to invite them to visit. Suggest a week that might work well. If you get no reply, follow up with a phone call.

2 **Plan carefully.** Decide how long each person will get to speak (make sure it is the same for everyone) and how long you will have for asking questions. Plan where the vote will take place, how everyone will cast their vote, and who will count the votes. How will you make sure the process is fair?

3  **Write questions in advance**. Candidates will probably want to talk about lots of issues besides climate change, so it's a good idea to prepare some questions that you would definitely like answered. Research each candidate and their party's policy on the climate emergency. You can ask them to send their campaign leaflets—then ask questions that they didn't answer in the material. Here are some ideas.

Are you doing everything in your power to fight the climate emergency?

What is your party's policy on energy and the environment?

What new policies would you put in place to act on climate change?

How will climate change affect our area?

What are you doing yourself to cut greenhouse gas emissions?

4   **Keep a record**. Task someone with keeping notes during the event and someone else with taking photos. You could invite the local press, too, and share the results of the mock vote.

5   **Stay in touch**. Write to thank the candidates after the visit. You could ask them to support a particular campaign at your school. The support of people in power can be very important in getting things done. Follow up each time you have something new to report, or to ask about your visitors' progress in doing the things they talked about.

# LIVE
# S-L-O-W-L-Y

Too busy to read
this page? Then
you \*have\* to read
this page.

## PLANET-O-METER

We use machines powered by fossil fuels to speed up our lives: cars to travel faster, gadgets to wash clothes more quickly, digital devices to send information at two-thirds of the speed of light. In 1930, a famous economist predicted that machines would save us so much time in the future, we'd need to work for only three hours a day. But he was wrong. Fast-forward 90 years, and we're cramming more than ever into each day.

Figure out how long you spend at school each week. Then add the time you spend on homework, sports, music, and other organized activities. It's easy to see why sometimes you have to jump in the car or grab a bottle of water on the go, just to get everything done, right? The pressure we put on ourselves also puts pressure on the planet.

Now a whole movement is embracing the power of living slowly. Research suggests that the following activities are not only good for our mental well-being but also good for the environment. The less you try to pack into each day, the less you'll consume—and the more space you'll have to plan ahead and live in a sustainable way.

# COUNTDOWN TO LIFE IN THE SLOW LANE

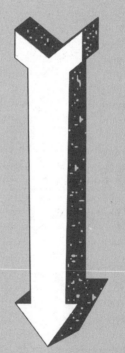

3. **Travel slow.** Try to travel by foot (or scooter or bike) whenever possible. For longer journeys, use public transportation.

2. **Talk slow.** Try to check emails and social media messages only twice a day, and focus on face-to-face chats instead. A survey of 540,000 teenagers in 72 countries found that teenagers who spent some time eating or "just talking" with their families every day were more satisfied with their lives.

1. **Think slow.** The internet gives us instant answers to our questions, but we could be at risk of information overload. Teenagers who spend more than six hours a day online say they feel less satisfied with their lives. Swap some of your scrolling time for the slow pleasure of reading a good book.

# SUSS OUT THE SCIENCE SUPERPOWERS

Keep studying science, technology, engineering, and math, and you could start suggesting new solutions.

**PLANET-O-METER**

Many scientists agree that we can minimize the effects of global warming if we can keep the concentration of carbon dioxide in the atmosphere at a safe level. But in 2019, the level started getting dangerously high, and it's still rising. To bring it back down, we'll have to cut emissions **AND** try to recapture some of the extra greenhouse gases that have already been released.

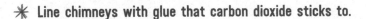

How would you do it?

* Line chimneys with glue that carbon dioxide sticks to.
* Use toothpaste as a sunscreen for the planet.
* Build a giant umbrella in space to shade us from the sun.
* Snack on jellyfish chips.

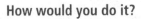

Amazingly, these are all real solutions being considered by scientists and engineers! Chemists at the Energy Safety Research Institute (ESRI) at Swansea University in Wales have created a special carbon capture material using a type of glue found in most homes.

Scientists based at Harvard University are designing a sunshade, using balloons to release tiny particles of calcium carbonate (one of the main ingredients in toothpaste) into the atmosphere to reflect sunlight back into space and cool the planet. Could it work? Well, we know that when a huge volcano erupted in 1991, the particles of sulfur dioxide it released cooled the planet by almost 1°F for about 18 months. Toothpaste is **WAY** less stinky.

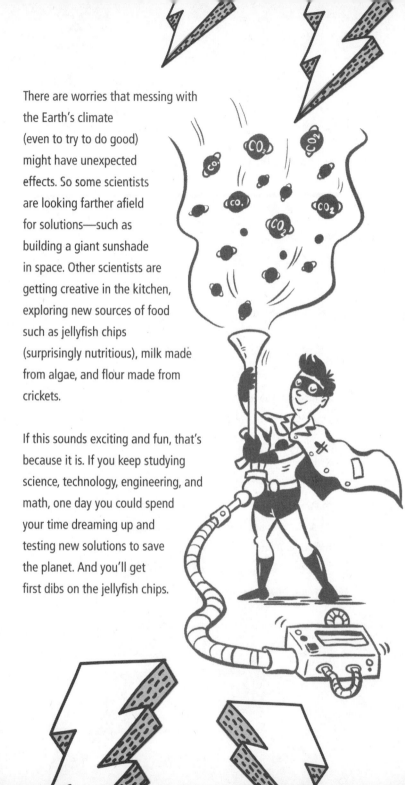

There are worries that messing with the Earth's climate (even to try to do good) might have unexpected effects. So some scientists are looking farther afield for solutions—such as building a giant sunshade in space. Other scientists are getting creative in the kitchen, exploring new sources of food such as jellyfish chips (surprisingly nutritious), milk made from algae, and flour made from crickets.

If this sounds exciting and fun, that's because it is. If you keep studying science, technology, engineering, and math, one day you could spend your time dreaming up and testing new solutions to save the planet. And you'll get first dibs on the jellyfish chips.

# GIVE SIGHTS, SOUNDS, AND SENSATIONS ... NOT STUFF!

Do you think you're good at choosing gifts? Think again. Science shows we're choosing all the wrong things!

**PLANET-O-METER**

More than three-quarters of us give objects that can be wrapped, but psychologists based in Canada have discovered that **EXPERIENCES** make far better gifts. People are more likely to react emotionally to experiences, from a 😮 sport to a 😎 day trip to a 🙁 movie. These types of gifts make people feel closer to the giver. Happily, these are the kinds of gifts that make the planet smile, too.

## 10 EXPERIENCES TO GIVE (OR ASK FOR)

1. TICKETS TO A MOVIE, SHOW, OR EXHIBITION

2. A VISIT TO A PLACE LINKED TO A FAVORITE HOBBY

3. A SESSION AT THE BATTING CAGES OR A ROUND OF MINI GOLF

4. A TRAIN TICKET TO VISIT A NEW PLACE

5. AN APP THAT TEACHES A NEW SKILL, SUCH AS STARGAZING

6. A VOUCHER FOR A FUN ACTIVITY, SUCH AS INDOOR CLIMBING

★

★

★

★
★

7. SOMETHING YOU OWN BUT DON'T USE AND THAT STILL WORKS, SUCH AS A CAMERA

8. A BIKE RENTAL IN A PARK

9. A TICKET TO A SPORTING EVENT OR CONCERT

10. A CAMPING TRIP

Expensive surprises aren't any good either—
scientists in the United States have found that
people prefer cheaper, more practical gifts.
So next time you're getting a gift for someone,
tell them you'd like to get them an experience
and ask what they'd like to do.

# OPEN A
# MUSEUM

Entrance fee:
a pledge to help
save the planet!

## PLANET-O-METER

Instead of visiting a museum, ask if your class
or community group can set up its own. Plan
a **MUSEUM OF CLIMATE CHANGE** event and invite
the whole school community. Appoint different
classmates to curate the exhibition, advertise
the event, issue tickets, act as gallery
attendants, and even collect donations
to put toward a climate action project.

Several places around the world have their own museums devoted to climate change, including Hong Kong, Rio de Janeiro, New York, and Oslo.

**Your exhibits could include:**

    ✳ Info that explains the past, present, and future
        of the climate emergency

    ✳ Everyday items that are climate change culprits

    ✳ Safer, greener alternatives

    ✳ Short films or animations you have made

    ✳ Arts and crafts projects to raise awareness

    ✳ Interactive exhibits, with activities like making
        draft stoppers (see page 161)

Create a short information card about each exhibit and assign "staff" to stand next to the exhibits to give visitors more information. Ask visitors to complete a short survey on their way out to share what they learned about climate change.

Can you really make a museum out of recycling? YES! When Robert Opie was 16, he began collecting packaging that would normally be thrown away. He held his first exhibition in 1975. His collection grew and eventually became the Museum of Brands in London.

# CLEAR OUT THE CLUTTER

We hate to say it, but . . . it's time to clean your room.

**PLANET-O-METER**

Is your bedroom overflowing with broken toys, games you've grown out of, and gadgets you never use? Tidying up may seem like a one-way ticket to boredom, but the benefits may change your mind. Psychologists have found that people who think their homes are cluttered also feel more stressed. Clearing out chaos can make you calmer and happier. It may even make you more creative. Researchers discovered that children play **MORE** creatively when they have **FEWER** toys to choose from. Clutter seems to distract us from doing things we enjoy and care about.

So where does climate change come in? Clearing out clutter does two things: It redistributes what you don't need so that others can reuse it. And it shows you that you can live with less, which could inspire you to buy less in the future. It can feel hard—we all get attached to our stuff. Break the process into steps to help.

---

**Worldwide, people spend more than $85 billion on traditional toys and games every year.**

---

# COUNTDOWN TO DECLUTTERING YOUR BEDROOM

5. Make space for two piles in your bedroom—one for things you absolutely have to keep and one for things that you feel happy to donate (including anything that doesn't fit or that you've outgrown in other ways).

4. Turn decluttering into a game. On day one, choose one object to put in the donate pile. On day two, pick two objects, and so on. How far can you get?

3. Make a separate pile of things that are broken. Turn to page 27 to see if you can find a way to repair them.

2. Time for the feel-good part—choose where you will send the donate pile. You could try freecycling websites and groups (ask an adult to help), local thrift stores, collection banks, families with younger children, school libraries, playgroups, or medical waiting rooms. There are also lots of apps for selling pre-loved clothes and toys—ask an adult if they can sell things for you.

1. Finally, sort your "absolutely have to keep pile" into things you use often and things you use more rarely. Hide the "use rarely" pile away for a few weeks, and then reassess. Is there anything you could now donate?

# HACK YOUR HOME

Try these tricks to cut energy use and make your home more climate friendly.

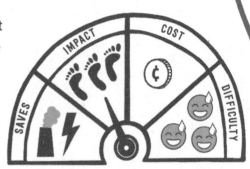

**PLANET-O-METER**

Time for some good news: in the United States, greenhouse gas emissions in 2018 were 10.2 percent lower than 2005 levels. Some of the shift was thanks to businesses and households finding ways to use less electricity. This is something **YOU** can help with.

Just over a third of the reduction was due to a shift to "cleaner" electricity, generated using natural gas and renewables instead of coal. (Natural gas is a fossil fuel, but burning natural gas releases less than two-thirds of the carbon dioxide released by burning coal.)

**1** **Vanquish vampires.** You won't need garlic. These vampires are devices that slowly suck electricity even when turned off. To stop them in their tracks, unplug computers, televisions, microwaves, and other devices when not in use.

**2** **Switch to the small screen.** Most of us love to sit in front of the television, and the bigger the TV, the more power it uses. Plasma TVs also use more energy than LCD screens. If you have a choice, watch on the smallest screen in the house. Turn the brightness and contrast down, too. It's an easy way to use less power, it could save your family up to $127 a year, and it might even make the picture look better.

**3** **Stop drying clothes on the radiator.** It keeps the radiator from playing its part in heating the house, forcing the boiler to work harder to make up for it. If it's a nice day, try hanging clothes near an open window instead. (This saves on the need for ironing too!)

**4** **Adjust the thermostat by 1 degree.** Heating and air-conditioning are the biggest uses of energy in most homes, and demand is increasing in some parts of the world because of extreme weather conditions. Turning the thermostat up 1 degree (if you're cooling the house) or down 1 degree (if you're heating the house) is a tiny change that makes a massive difference.

**5** **Turn off the lights.**

Okay, you can turn them on again.

# PARK AND STRIDE

What would you do if you discovered that the air in your school was anything but fresh?

**PLANET-O-METER**

You'd probably want to do something about it—especially as you're expected to breathe it all day, every day, while putting your brain through its paces. Shockingly, the Environmental Protection Agency has found that indoor levels of pollutants may be two to five times—and sometimes more than 100 times—as high as levels outdoors. This means that millions of schoolchildren are breathing in tiny toxic particles that increase their risk of asthma and other health problems.

Traffic outside schools is one of the main causes of this air pollution. It includes exhaust fumes from the cars that idle around school at drop-off and pickup times. These cars don't just drop off students—they leave behind exhaust fumes that hang around playgrounds and paths.

# RETHINK THE TRIP TO SCHOOL

1 Take part in national or regional walk- or bike-to-school initiatives, like Walk to School Day in October. If that goes well, try a regular program to encourage more people to leave the car at home. This could include an informal walking group (set up by parents) or a formal walking bus (set up by your school), which follows a set route collecting new "passengers" on the way. Or you could join in with a "walk once a week" plan such as WOW (Walk on Wednesdays) or Friday Footsteps in the United Kingdom. Some schools offer a reward to anyone who walks or bikes, such as a free piece of fruit.

**2** Help families who live farther from school take part. This might include carpooling or park-and-stride programs, where the school arranges for parents to use a local parking lot each morning and afternoon and walk the last 10 minutes to school. You could even suggest that a walking bus or group pass by the parking lot. The Department of Transportation's Safe Routes to Schools Programs has everything your school needs to get started: www.transportation.gov /mission/health/Safe-Routes-to-School -Programs.

**3** Persuade parents to change their behavior. Lots of schools have found that student-led campaigns can really make a difference. This includes things like closing roads near the school for a day and even issuing parking tickets to parents. You'll need your teachers' help to do anything like this—never approach parents or cars on your own. Find out what other schools are doing, and take some ideas in to show your teacher.

# TACKLE CARBON PAWPRINTS

Pets may be cute, but they're leaving behind something gross.

## PLANET-O-METER

And it's not what you think! Cats and dogs have a catastrophic carbon pawprint. The United States is the biggest pet-owning nation, and its 163 million dogs and cats are responsible for as many greenhouse gas emissions as 13.5 million cars. Just like the cars, it's not their fault. It's up to their owners to take steps to shrink them. (The emissions, not the pets.)

The biggest problem is their meaty (and fishy) diets. Producing cat and dog food is thought to be responsible for at least one-quarter of the environmental impact of animal farming in the United States. This is set to rise as more people around the world choose to own pets and to feed them better-quality meat.

# COUNTDOWN TO CUTTING CARBON PAWPRINTS

5. If you don't have a pet yet, **consider not getting one.** (Offer to take a friend's dog for walks or to care for it when they're away.)

4. **Always adopt a pet** instead of buying one. You could choose a vegetarian pet, such as a guinea pig.

3. **Feed them green grub.** Ask a vet for advice on switching your pet to a less meaty diet. In some countries, there are dog foods on the market made from combinations of insects, grains, root vegetables, and even fungi.

2. **Reduce.** All the advice in this book works for your pet, too. Buy things that last, avoid single-use plastic (hunt out biodegradable poop bags), and look for secondhand toys, scratching posts, and beds.

1. **Reuse and recycle.** Make your own pet toys— there are lots of ideas online, and since they're free or cheap to create, you can change the toys more often to keep your pet entertained. You could even make your own cat litter using shredded newspaper or junk mail.

# BE ANNOYING

Don't be afraid to pester people in power.

## PLANET-O-METER

Taking on both world leaders and business leaders, Greta Thunberg has made headlines for speaking truth to power. At the United Nations Climate Action Summit in 2019, she asked world leaders, "How dare you continue to look away and come here saying that you're doing enough, when the politics and solutions needed are still nowhere in sight?"

You probably won't bump into world leaders very often, but you **CAN** tell your local politicians what you think. Start by finding out who your district's representative to Congress is. Members of Congress are elected to represent the interests and concerns of their constituents (the people who live in a certain region). Even though you can't vote

yet, you are still a constituent, so let your representative know about your concerns. The best way to do this is in writing. On page 159, you'll find a template letter to get you started.

Members of Congress are responsible for debating and voting on new national laws. The questions they raise, the votes they take, and the legislation they support on your behalf can make a big difference. Once a law has been passed, the responsibility for putting it into action may lie with local governments, so getting in touch with local politicians can make a difference too. Ask your teacher to help find out who your local politicians are, and use the tips on page 126 to invite them to talk to your class and answer your questions. Remember to ask how **YOU** can get involved in local politics yourself one day!

# LETTERS FOR CHANGE

**Use the template letter on page 159 to begin writing your own letter to a politician.**

**PLANET-O-METER**

You can adapt this to write to anyone in power at the local, state, or national level. To help your letter stand out, keep it short (one side of one page), be polite, and include your name and school address so the recipient can see that you are their constituent. As with any piece of writing, start with **RESEARCH**. Find out as much as you can about the issue you are concerned about, the science behind it, and whether the politician has already done any work linked to it.

Remember to end your letter by asking the person to take **ACTION**— the more specific, the better! For example, would you like them to bring something up in Congress or raise it with the government department responsible for climate change? To vote in a particular way on a proposed new law? To help you campaign on a local issue? Or to do something else?

The larger the district a politician represents, the more constituents they will have. For the average member of the US House of Representatives, this is 747,000 people. They may get thousands of letters every day. But they say that personal letters (or emails) really do make a difference. The more letters and emails they receive, the better they will understand what matters to their constituents.

[Your address]

[Their address]

[Date]

**Dear** [Name and title]:

**I am writing to you about the climate emergency. We urgently need to reduce greenhouse gas emissions in our country and around the world.**

[Add a few sentences about your personal story (see page 180) and what you are especially worried about. How does climate change affect you and your local area now, or how will it affect you in the future? Let the recipient know about any actions you are taking yourself.

You could also mention any scientific findings or headlines that have worried you.

Ask them to take action on this issue. (Be specific!)]

**I look forward to hearing back from you.**

**Sincerely,**

[Your name]

# HOW TO GET IN TOUCH

Ask an adult to help you find the right postal or email address. Most countries have special websites with listings, for example:

**US:**
**HOUSE.GOV/REPRESENTATIVES/FIND-YOUR -REPRESENTATIVE**

**AUSTRALIA:**
**APH.GOV.AU/SENATORS_AND_MEMBERS/GUIDELINES _FOR_CONTACTING_SENATORS_AND_MEMBERS**

**UK:**
**MEMBERS.PARLIAMENT.UK**

# FILL YOUR HOME WITH SNAKES

Not real ones! These rag reptiles only prey on drafts.

**PLANET-O-METER**

Picture this. You're snuggled up on the sofa, remote control in one hand, popcorn in the other, ready to hit play. Suddenly something **COLD** and **UNWELCOME** sends a shiver down your spine. Drafts are those annoying currents of cold air that waft through rooms, making the air feel colder than it really is. Drafts mean warm air is escaping from our homes, making us reach for the thermostat, nudging up our energy use even further.

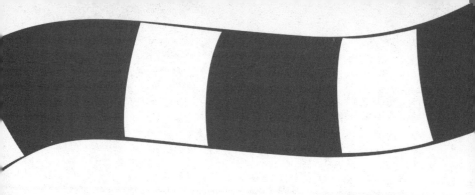

Draft-proofing is your secret weapon in saving energy, and the easiest way to do it is to fill the house with snakes. These serpent-shaped draft stoppers are easy to make, using things that you might otherwise throw away, and they're perfect for blocking small gaps under windows and doors. For stuffing, you can use anything you have around the house. Use a mixture of **HEAVY** things (such as rice, dried beans, peas, or corn) and **SOFT, FLUFFY** things (such as scrap packaging from deliveries, the insides of an old pillow or cushion, worn-out tights and socks, used plastic bags, or a rolled-up blanket).

Energy Star estimates that US households could save up to 10 percent of their total annual energy bills by ~~making novelty snakes~~ sealing and insulating air leaks.

## SEW A SNAKE

1   Cut one leg off a worn pair of pants or tights.
    (Ask a parent first. Especially if they're wearing
    the pants or tights.)

2   Tie one end with a strip of fabric or a scrap of string
    or ribbon.

3   Fill the leg with stuffing, packing it really tightly.

4   Tie the end.

5   Glue or sew on button eyes and a red ribbon or
    fabric tongue.

## SUPERQUICK STUFFY SNAKE

Do you have loads of stuffed animals you can't bear to part with?
Give them a job saving the planet! Simply line them up
with their backs against a door or wall. Then use safety pins to join
them together to make a soft toy "snake."

**Don't block holes that are supposed to be
there, such as vents and exhaust fans. They
keep the air in our homes fresh and healthy.**

# MARCH FOR THE CLIMATE

Would you like to protest in person? Don't leave home without reading these tips!

## PLANET-O-METER

Since Greta Thunberg's first protest outside the Swedish parliament (see page 41), thousands of young people in more than 1,500 cities around the world have joined climate marches, protests, and strikes. If you are planning to participate, read this first so you go prepared.

## COUNTDOWN TO A MEANINGFUL MARCH

5. **Know what you're marching for.**
   People have responded very differently
   to the news that thousands of children
   are taking action for the climate. In one
   English school, the principal asked
   students questions to prove they knew
   what they were marching for. Read
   up on the event and the issues it is
   drawing attention to before you show up.

4. **Plan carefully.** Many climate change protests are planned as peaceful and quiet protests, and some (such as many #FridaysforFuture events) seek police approval in advance. The organizers should help by providing details on a website or flyer. Research where they plan to meet, what people will do once they are there (for example, walking along a planned route, taking part in activities, or listening to speeches and music), and how they plan to keep protesters safe (for example, by arranging for roads to be closed).

3. **Invite your friends and family.** Never go to a protest alone. Taking an adult along with you will help keep you safe—and anyway, the more people who show up, the louder the message. So invite friends and family to join you.

2. **Make a poster.** A protest sign helps you share your message with the world. Create yours from recycled materials, and try to make it rainproof. Find out if there are any rules for the event you are attending—some don't allow signs on sticks. Keep your message short and snappy so you can write it big—that way it will be seen from a distance.

1. **Stay safe.** Plan how you will travel to and from the protest and what you will do if you get separated from your friends and family. If the crowd is very large, cell phones may not work as well as usual. You might be standing for a long time, so wear comfortable shoes and dress for the weather. Remember to take water, snacks, and any medicines you need. When any large group gathers, unexpected things can sometimes happen. Stick close together, and be prepared to leave if some people aren't behaving peacefully.

# SWAP YOUR STUFF

Free stuff?
Yes, please!

IMPACT COST

SAVES

DIFFICULTY

0

**PLANET-O-METER**

It feels good to get something new, but the feeling doesn't last for long. Psychologists have found that the joy fades away over as few as **FIVE** days. Soon a new toy or game catches our eye, and the cycle repeats itself. The cost to the planet is huge.

To get that new-to-you feeling without hurting your piggy bank or your planet, try organizing a swap party or event. It could reduce waste that might otherwise end up in a landfill, help you declutter your bedroom (see page 141), **AND** cut the amount of greenhouse gases released in the manufacture of new stuff.

169

1 **Pick a location** with a large captive audience, such as school or the meeting place of a group that you belong to. You'll need a room large enough to lay things out with space for people to walk around and "shop." You'll need to recruit several adult helpers, too.

2 **Set the ground rules.** For example, you could ask that all donated toys, books, and games be clean and unbroken, with no missing pieces. You could also ask people to avoid donating electric or battery-powered toys (or at least remove the batteries first).

3  **Decide on a system.** Reuse scrap materials to make tokens, which will work like money at the event. You may want to issue one token per toy, so each person can choose the same number of toys they donated. But it's not fair to swap a scooter for a stuffed animal! You could ask someone like a teacher or parent to decide on the value of each item, and issue tokens accordingly.

4  **Spread the word.** Make posters and ask if your event can be featured in school or local newsletters. Include information about when and where to take toys for tagging, and when to turn up for the swap itself. Remember to ask people to bring their own bags to carry their swaps away in.

5  **Ready, set, swap!** On the day of the event, leave plenty of time for checking donations, making sure they are clean and safe, and tagging them with a "price." You could designate a certain table for each price—for example, 2 tokens, 5 tokens, 10 tokens. This is quicker than tagging each toy, but you'll need someone at each table to collect the tokens. If items are left at the end, you can donate them or save them for a future swap event.

READY, SET, SWAP!

# LEAD BY EXAMPLE

Are leaders born
or made?

**PLANET-O-METER**

Research shows that everyone has the potential to develop leadership skills. Taking action on something you care about—like climate change—can be a great way to get started.

Start by brainstorming all the things that make you **YOU**! If you're not sure what to write, try cutting pictures and words from old magazines and newspapers to make a collage that represents you. Then scribble down all the qualities from your collage that could make a difference in your work on climate change. Are you excellent at doing research, talented at telling stories, or good at making arts and crafts? Brainstorm ways you could put your special skills and qualities to work to raise awareness about environmental issues. This exercise might help you pick which suggestions in this book you'd like to try.

Next, write the names of some people you could tell about each idea and maybe even ask for help or support. Now you have a plan. Finally, take a deep breath, get out there, and start sharing your ideas. Lead by example, and you'll inspire other people to follow in your footsteps without having to boss them around. This is leadership—you are doing it!

# HUNT FOR YOUR HERO

With so many ways to help the planet, where should you start? Take a tip from other young climate activists and be guided by your interests and skills.

**PLANET-O-METER**

Young activists are making headlines around the world with their action against climate change. Complete the quiz on the next page to find out which eco-hero you have the most in common with, and then find out how they got started.

1 **What is one aspect of climate change you feel very concerned about?**
   a) Climate injustice—when the effects of climate change (and the responsibility for tackling it) are not fairly shared
   b) The increased risk of devastating famines
   c) Extreme weather events
   d) The impact on the world's oceans and marine wildlife

2 **What special talents or skills do you have?**
   a) Theater skills and singing
   b) Giving speeches in front of lots of people
   c) Physical strength, developed through things like sports and rock climbing
   d) Technical skills, such as making videos

3 **What gives you hope?**
   a) Seeing young people realize how powerful they can be
   b) Witnessing people put the climate above their own desires
   c) Being part of positive action, like a rally
   d) Discovering simple things I can do that make a difference

4 **What is one change you would like to see?**
   a) 100 percent renewable energy by 2030
   b) News sites reporting more on the climate crisis than on celebrities
   c) An end to new coal, oil, and gas projects
   d) People leading sustainable lives and creating less waste

**Mostly As**

**Your climate hero might be . . . Noga Levy-Rapoport**

Noga lives in England, where she juggles her schoolwork with helping lead the UK Student Climate Network. As a young climate activist, she campaigns for politicians to take climate change more seriously. In addition to writing articles and speaking at rallies and on the radio, Noga has helped organize the school strike for climate marches in the United Kingdom and has led a protest march in London.

**Mostly Bs**

**Your climate hero might be . . . Leah Namugerwa**

Leah lives in Uganda, a country where the higher average temperatures caused by global warming are leading to more severe droughts and the desertification of farmland. Leah was inspired to take action when she was 12 and saw news reports about a famine affecting millions of people in the north of her country. Leah takes part in school strikes through Fridays for Future Uganda and has organized a petition to ban plastic bags in Uganda. She also leads by example, planting 200 trees for her 15th birthday instead of having a party.

### Mostly Cs
### Your climate hero might be . . .
### Harriet O'Shea Carre

With her friends Milou Albrecht and Callum Neilson-Bridgefoot, Harriet started the Australian School Strike 4 Climate (SS4C) movement in 2018. They led the first strike outside their local member of Parliament's office, demanding an end to new fossil fuel projects and a commitment to 100 percent renewable energy by 2030. Harriet says that talking to politicians is out of her comfort zone but that it's worth it to try to get people to take action for a safe planet. She was invited to share her vision at the United Nations Youth Climate Summit.

### Mostly Ds
### Your climate hero might be . . .
### Dylan D'Haeze

Dylan lives in Washington State. He was 13 when he first became aware of the huge problems caused by plastic waste in the world's oceans. At first, he felt worried, but he decided to tackle his worries by asking questions and learning how to make movies to share the answers he discovered. Since then, Dylan has made a series of documentaries to share the problems of climate change with other children around the world. You can watch them at **kidscansavetheplanet.com**.

These stories show there is more than **ONE** way to fight for the climate. Start with the issues that concern you most, and think about how you can use your unique talents and skills to share the message—and inspire people to find solutions.

# DON'T TRY TO BE PERFECT

It's better to take small steps than to do nothing at all.

PLANET-O-METER

The best leaders don't expect to get their own way all the time, and they don't want to. Instead, they share their vision and ideas and then listen carefully to other people. They hope to inspire others to have their own ideas and take action too.

What should you do if someone criticizes your ideas? Climate activists find this can happen, partly because taking action means making changes to the way we live. Some of these changes will be inconvenient—for individuals, for businesses, and for people in power. But climate scientists want us to start thinking differently. They argue that short-term inconveniences are nothing compared to the risks of overheating our planet.

By researching the science behind climate change and potential solutions, you can listen to other points of view but be confident in your own understanding and ideas. Most importantly, don't feel that you have to live a perfect, zero-carbon life before you can start encouraging other people to take action. Sometimes famous climate change activists are criticized for doing things that use fossil fuels, such as taking flights. There is no such thing as a truly zero-carbon life at the moment, but that doesn't mean we should stop working toward it. It's far better to have millions of people taking action imperfectly than to have just a handful trying to live a zero-carbon life while everyone else does nothing.

# SHARE
# A STORY

Once upon a time
there was a planet
that was not too hot,
not too cold, but
just right. . . .

IMPACT

COST

SAVES

DIFFICULTY

PLANET-O-METER

The science of climate change is really important. Gathering huge amounts of data over a vast area and thousands of years is the only way to fully understand what is happening. But stories can tell us why climate change **MATTERS**.

Many people respond more emotionally to stories than to statistics, so storytelling can be a powerful way to connect with people about climate change.

If you're excellent at entertaining people with anecdotes or great at building suspense, consider using your storytelling skills to tackle the climate emergency.

Stories get people talking. Two not-for-profit organizations—the Environmental Defense Fund and the Hunger Project—made a Bollywood-style film called *Aarohan* about the challenges of climate change for rural communities in India, such as access to food and water. The movie is being used to get communities talking about ideas for fighting climate change.

GET TALKING

## 5 IDEAS FOR FIGHTING CLIMATE CHANGE WITH STORYTELLING

1   **What's your story?** When did you first learn
    about climate change, and how did it
    make you feel? What are you doing to make
    a difference? How have your efforts made you
    feel? Practice telling your story orally, in
    writing, or in another creative way—for
    example, as a cartoon or comic strip.

2   **Tell the story of climate change in your
    own words.** It's epic. Who and what are
    the villains? Who will be the heroes?

3  **Dig out local stories.** Climate change is a global problem, which can often mean numbers so big that they're hard to understand or care about. Talking about the impact of climate change on people, plants, and animals that live in the immediate area can make someone sit up and listen.

4  **Share happy stories, too.** The stories of climate change that make headlines often leave us feeling scared, frustrated, or powerless. But people are more likely to take action if they feel hopeful. When you read a story about positive action by an individual, an organization, or a government, share it with others.

5  **Start a new chapter.** Remember that the story of climate change is still being written, and you get to help decide how it ends.

# GREEN, SLEEP, REPEAT

Climate action isn't just about breaking bad habits . . .

**PLANET-O-METER**

. . . it's about forming new ones that last for life. Some of the changes in this book (like rewilding a yard) are one-off projects. But most are small changes to the way you live that will help you help the planet forever. Luckily, science tells us how to form a habit that lasts.

1  **Give yourself a cue**. Tack a new task onto
   something you **ALREADY** do every day, and it
   will soon become automatic too. For example,
   you could decide that each time you head to the
   bathroom to brush your teeth, you will turn off
   every switch and device you pass on the way.

2  **Take two months.** Scientists at University College London studied 96 different people and found that they took an average of 66 days to form a new habit. Expect it to take this long to make a new habit part of your life. Don't try to make 50 changes at once, or it might be your brain that overheats!

3  **Don't worry if you miss a day.** The same study also found that slipping up didn't stop people from forming a habit if they just kept going as normal afterward. Having a barbecued burger or taking a car to school because it's pouring rain doesn't mean you've failed. It means you're on the right path—you've started to notice what you do and the impact your actions have on the environment.

# IF THE PLANET HAD ANOTHER 7.7 BILLION PEOPLE **LIKE YOU,** ITS PROBLEMS WOULD BE **SOLVED.**

# INDEX

## A

acidification, 71
aerosols, 49
Amazon rain forest, 66
Antarctica, 14, 15, 16, 50
Arctic, 14
atmosphere, 10, 12, 15, 16, 17, 18,
    22, 51, 65, 66, 69, 71, 72, 73, 74,
    75, 87, 106, 107, 132, 133

## B

bathing, 47, 48
batteries, 115–118, 170
beef, 23, 34, 35, 81, 82, 83, 102
bicycles/cycling, 53, 123, 131, 150
borrowing and lending, 111

## C

carbon calculators, 57
carbon capture, 65, 72, 133
carbon dioxide, 11, 12, 16, 17, 18, 23,
    51, 57, 65, 66, 71, 72, 73, 74, 87,
    132, 133, 144
carbon footprint, 22, 31, 44, 46, 52,
    55, 58, 59, 62, 63, 69, 72, 76, 80,
    93, 94, 97, 105, 110, 122, 152,
    154
carbon-neutral, 57, 72, 115
carbon offsetting, 73
cars, 27, 42, 99, 115, 122, 124, 129,
    148, 151, 152
central heating, 17, 44, 46,
    48, 146

chlorofluorocarbons (CFCs), 49–50
chocolate, 22, 23, 81
climate (definition), 73
clothes
    carbon footprint of, 76, 77
    drying, 146
    labels, 97
    recycling, 97, 98, 143
    repairing, 28, 76, 78, 79
    washing, 47, 129
    See also fast fashion
CO$_2$e (definition), 73
cycling (see bicycles)

## D

deforestation, 17, 73, 106
D'Haeze, Dylan, 177
digital devices, 109, 116, 129
dishwasher, 47
draft stoppers, 161–164
drought, 21, 114, 176

## E

election, mock, 125–128
electric heaters, 44
electricity, 17, 44, 55, 57, 74, 109,
    115, 118, 144, 145
emissions, 18, 23, 27, 44, 46, 55, 57,
    59, 63, 73, 74, 76, 77, 80, 93, 97,
    100, 104, 105, 106, 108, 115, 127,
    132, 144, 152, 159
energy-efficient homes, 44, 46, 47,
    48, 55, 62, 144–146, 161–164

**F**

fast fashion, 95
fertilizers, 37, 89, 90
flexitarianism, 84, 85
food, 24, 25–26, 81
   labels, 104–107
   miles, 22–24
   packaging, 25, 59
   waste, 59–61
fossil fuels, 17, 44, 59, 69, 72, 74,
   106, 179

**G**

gardening, 36–37, 39, 66
glaciers, 14
global warming (definition), 74
greenhouse effect (definition), 74
greenhouse gases, 12, 17, 18, 22,
   28, 44, 50, 55, 69, 72, 73, 74, 82,
   107, 132
   *See also* emissions

**H**

hydrofluorocarbons, 50

**I**

ice cores, 15, 16
ice sheets, 14, 15, 19, 21, 114
Industrial Revolution, 17
insects, 38

**L**

landfill, 28, 68, 70, 169
lending and borrowing, 32, 33–35
Levy-Rapoport, Noga, 176
livestock, 80, 107

**M**

marches, 165, 166–168
mass extinction, 86, 87, 88
meat, 80, 81, 82, 84, 85, 102, 107
   pet diet, 153, 154
methane, 11, 12, 16, 17, 44, 87

**N**

Namugerwa, Leah, 176
nitrous oxide, 11, 12, 16, 17

**O**

O'Shea Carre, Harriet, 177
oceans, 65, 75, 71, 177

**P**

palm oil, 106
Paris Climate Agreement, 65
park and stride, 151
pesticides, 37
petitions, 113, 176
petroleum oil, 69
   *See also* fossil fuels
pets, 152–154
planned obsolescence, 27, 28, 95
plastic, 39, 68, 69, 70, 177
   bags, 162, 176
   recycling, 69
   reuse, 39, 162
   single-use, 70, 103, 154
politicians
   letter to, 155–160
protests, 167
   *See also* marches

## R

recycling, 68–70, 103, 140, 154, 168
renewable energy, 44, 75, 99, 115, 144, 177
    *See also* solar power
repair café, 31, 120, 123
repairing goods, 28, 30–31
ride-sharing, 124

## S

School Strike for Climate (SS4C), 41, 176, 177
screen time, 92–94
single-use plastic, 70, 103, 154
solar power, 62, 75, 99, 115
staycations, 52–53
swapping, 169–171
swishing party, 98

## T

temperature, 10, 12, 13, 14, 15, 21, 73, 74, 114, 176
Thunberg, Greta, 40–43, 113, 155, 165
trains, 42, 53, 101, 124

## V

vacations, 52, 124
veganism, 85
vegetarianism, 43, 84, 85
    meat-free Mondays, 102
    pet diet, 154
volcanic eruption, 87, 133

## W

water, 14, 23, 44, 46, 48, 67, 71, 80
water vapor, 11, 12
weather (definition), 75
well-being
    mental, 92, 114, 130
    physical, 80, 84, 148
wildlife, 38, 39, 71

# MORE WAYS TO BE AN ECO-WARRIOR!

ISABEL THOMAS

THIS BOOK IS NOT GARBAGE

**50** WAYS TO DITCH **PLASTIC**, REDUCE **TRASH**, AND **SAVE** THE **WORLD!**